THE SCIENCE OF HAPPY EMPLOYEES

THE
SCIENCE
OF HAPPY
EMPLOYEES

What it takes to have a psychosocially safe
workplace with happy and productive employees

Dr Brenda Jamnik

Following the merger of PNG Telikom and B-Mobile, Dr Brenda has undertaken the careful planning and commenced the challenging implementation of the key elements required for us to become a high-performance team. She has consulted across the business to prioritise the key features that describe our values and priorities and is working with the executives to adopt a new outcome-focused decision-making mindset. The executives have been positively responsive to her leadership and training.

Amos Tepi, CEO, Telikom Limited PNG

I have been working with Dr Brenda Jamnik over the last two years, developing and implementing collaborative project frameworks. She has a unique ability to evaluate the way we see opportunities and challenges and facilitates problem-solving in a pragmatic client-focused way. Brenda is adept at balancing what is needed with what is wanted, ensuring that everybody in the process feels included and heard. We continue to engage Brenda for her energy and ability to achieve outcomes under tight time constraints.

Mark Barrows, Project Director Fitzroy to Gladstone Pipeline, McConnell Dowell BMD JV

I have had the good fortune to have known and worked with Brenda on several projects spanning several years. Brenda's insights and ability to 'turn the telescope around' and view things from a different perspective are extraordinary – and she hits the bullseye on the target every time. I, for one, would be very happy to go up any hill with Brenda at any time and trust in her that 'we' would make it to the top.

Simon Latchford, Senior Manager, Economic Development, Tourism & Aviation

Dr Brenda has been working with us to improve our team knowledge and skills since 2016 and continues to work with us. She is focused on understanding what we need and always delivers outcomes greater than we expected. Dr Brenda's approach motivates us to think differently, which challenges us to become the best in leadership, learning, and development.

Dr Tituk Lestari, Head of Leadership Management, Competency Development Centre, Ministry of Home Affairs, Indonesia

Several years ago, I requested Brenda to provide me with some assistance on a large and complex water industry project. The project purpose was complex, multifaceted, and included elements that were applicable at different times, such as when there was either an excess or shortage of water. The project team was a group of people who were from different disciplines who were new to the organisation. I needed help aligning the team to a comprehensive and simple goal.

Brenda was invaluable due to her ability to think and look at a project as a living and responsive system. Using this perspective, she was able to help the team think from a full-system perspective and see where their element added to the outcome. Brenda is also acutely aware of the need for team alignment. Her insight into the psychology of individuals, complemented by her understanding and knowledge of leadership, enabled us to achieve a team that was fully aligned in support of the overall goal. The result was a high-performing, well-motivated, and fully aligned team. We were also able to clearly identify, understand, and explain to key stakeholders the whole-system objectives for the project.

Justin Cairns, Manager Government Projects; Operations; Water New South Wales

Dr Brenda Jamnik is a gifted educator and leader who has a natural conviction to produce consistent high-quality outcomes. I have witnessed this first-hand during Brenda's interactions with postgraduate students and business owners and managers who have participated in business micro-credential courses. On each occasion, Brenda develops a rapport and then guides the learners towards achieving their goals. Brenda demonstrates genuine concern for each learner and goes above and beyond, especially providing timely and meaningful feedback. Brenda epitomises professionalism, competence, intelligence, and generosity. I fully endorse Brenda as a credible, engaging, living legend who acts with integrity and compassion.

Dr Wayne Graham, Senior Lecturer, Management & Adjunct Senior Research Fellow, School of Business and Creative Industries, University of the Sunshine Coast

Dr Brenda has worked with me on multiple road projects to build a high-performing culture, ensuring that the foundations are set from the beginning to ensure successful delivery. She collaborates with us to build charters based on trust, respect, and empowerment, where psychological safety is a priority. Brenda guides us to set shared goals and KPIs, establish project values and behavioural expectations, and then coaches us to implement them. This means that we work like a well-oiled team and with clear guidance on how to manage the site relationships to ensure resolution of differences at the lowest level, with clear escalation processes. Brenda is an incredible mentor and coach and provides unique and innovative approaches when faced with relationship or culture challenges.

Gerard Vink, Project Manager Civil, FKG Group

I have had the privilege of working closely with Brenda for the past six years, and it has been an incredible journey. Our collaboration has spanned various aspects of my business, from business coaching and leadership development to shaping our organisational culture and providing invaluable insights at the board level. One of Brenda's most outstanding qualities is her unwavering commitment to excellence. She doesn't just go along with the status quo; she challenges, questions, and pushes the boundaries of our thinking, whether she agrees with our perspective or not. Brenda's ability to challenge our mindset, ideas, and actions has been instrumental in our growth. Thanks to her influence, our business has expanded fivefold in size, and I am immensely grateful for her contributions to this success. Brenda is a true visionary, and her unique perspective is something that sets her apart. Her brain operates in mysterious and extraordinary ways, consistently surprising me with her innovative ideas and ideologies. She has an uncanny ability to see opportunities where others may see challenges and to bring fresh, creative solutions to the table.

In summary, Brenda is one of a kind, and I can confidently say that her impact on my business and personal growth has been immeasurable. Her dedication, intellect, and exceptional ability to challenge the status quo have been pivotal in shaping our success. I look forward to continuing our partnership and benefiting from Brenda's brilliant insights in the years to come.

Stephen Rice, CEO, OzeIT

I have been very fortunate to have worked with Dr Brenda Jamnik on a number of projects, where her role has been that of a facilitator, drawing upon her many years of experience in developing and implementing strategies for government agencies and large private sector businesses in the development and building of systems through cultural and organisational change and relationship development. She brings with her a very high level of credibility and trust, and that, combined with attention to detail in her advice, brings about extraordinary results for those with whom she works.

Rick Jones, Consultant, JHK Legal

Working with Brenda and the SHEPS process was transformational for our Cyber Security company. We are a small company and had a leader who made others feel unsafe. The mention of staff feeling unsafe when answering the SHEPS questions honestly was the first indication that there was a deep cultural problem of which I was unaware. We have been working with Brenda and Org-CD and have taken action. The company is already seeing returns in customer contracts and commitment to innovation in employee results in just a few weeks. This was well worth it for us.

Kathryn Giudes, Independent Director, Founder & Managing Director MacroDATA

WHO IS DR BRENDA JAMNIK?

Dr Brenda Jamnik is a renowned leadership specialist who has received multiple awards. She has been invited to deliver workshops and speak at conferences in Australia and around the world. Dr Brenda is highly sought after for her expertise in coaching leaders to build high-performing teams that are psychosocially safe. The success of her approach is evident in the multiple national and international projects she has been involved in.

One notable project was her collaboration with the Education Department of Vanuatu. Through a Five Deep questioning process, Dr Brenda helped the participants understand the impact of student development on youth unemployment. They realised that the education system was focused on exam results rather than equipping students with the necessary competencies to contribute to the economy. This realisation led to a review and change in the curriculum offered in schools.

In her work with Water NSW, the owner and operator of the Warragamba Dam, Dr Brenda focused on aligning the purpose of the teams involved in the procurement process. This alignment was crucial in building a business case for major flood mitigation works. She developed leadership behavioural descriptors and an evaluation framework, and aligned them with the KPI framework and organisational values. Through multiple workshops, Dr Brenda observed high-performance team and leadership behaviours, team power dynamics and communication patterns. This process played a significant role in the selection of the successful contractor for the project.

Dr Brenda also coached a high-performance team that won the major category for projects at the Civil Contractors Federation Earth Awards. She supported the governance team on a $1.1B rail expansion project, ensuring effective decision making and a high-performance team. Her work involved aligning the three joint venture partners, managing contractor and client relationships, and achieving critical project drivers such as time, surety and value for money through a collaborative framework. Additionally, she conducted an appraisal of energy provider Alliance in Western Australia, identifying 68 areas for action that would improve efficiency and project return on investment for clients. All these areas for action were approved by the management committee, and strategies were developed for implementation.

Dr Brenda has served on multiple government and community advisory boards and professional organisations. She has a unique approach to achieving outcomes that others may deem unattainable. The testimonials at the front of her book, *The Science of Happy Employees*, reflect the exceptional standard of work she delivers and the outstanding results she helps achieve.

ACKNOWLEDGEMENTS

My deep gratitude to those who willingly gave of their time to answer my questions about their workplace practices, including Roz White, Rick Jones, Terry Cogill, Scott Baker, Stephen Rice, Zardi Tierney, Justin Cairns, Donna Niazov and the multiple other people who chose to speak with me and requested to remain anonymous; thank you.

Thank you, Andrew Griffiths, for the framework and mental challenges you provide – they are the essence and foundation that make this flow and become a reality.

Michael Hanrahan, this book would not be here without your support, mentorship and guidance; it is both appreciated and valued.

To our Deadline Keepers group and particularly Kerry Gibb for actually naming the book – thanks for your accountability, energy and laughter.

And to my somewhat patient husband Werner; although I think you are used to the ebbs and flows now, I am grateful for the support that you provide.

First published in 2024 by Brenda Jamnik

A catalogue entry for this book is available from the National Library of Australia.

ISBN: 978-1-923007-69-7

Printed in Australia by Pegasus
Book production and text design by Publish Central
Cover design by Julia Kuris

The paper this book is printed on is certified as environmentally friendly.

Disclaimer

CONTENTS

FOREWORD

Many small businesses fail for a number of reasons. In my experience observing, mentoring and co-investing there is a common thread among aspiring entrepreneurs – succinctly summarised, many don't know what they don't know. I equate setting up a business first time with being the captain of a ship. Get it right from day one or expect to run aground and lose it all.

I often find myself sitting in a coffee shop or restaurant keeping count of what's going on around me. I deal with service companies who deliver everything but service. I don't complain, rather I react in a way similar to many consumers: I don't go back. Over time that can lead to a fatal outcome – going broke.

One of the essential planks of a successful business is happy, loyal and committed colleagues. I use the latter terminology rather than 'staff' or 'employees' as your success will turn on the relationship you have with those in your employ.

There is little doubt in my successful business experience that building a healthy mental and social wellbeing culture within your organisation remains one of the significant strategic challenges confronting business owners. The problem is that many either don't recognise what is required or worse don't care. To get it right at times we need to unlearn old behaviours, past accepted norms and practices that nowadays don't cut it. We know safety but what do we know about psychological safety? Commentators remind us that there is a whole demographic of Australians beset by issues of anxiety, depression and lack of confidence.

The Science of Happy Employees is the go-to book for insights into what psychosocial safety is, where the hazards and mental health issues in the workplace might be lurking and some insights as to how to manage this.

This book has the capacity to help you get to the core of the issues and help build a cohort of happy colleagues and a productive workplace, both essential to a successful business.

I have known and worked with Brenda Jamnik over 40 years, commencing in Darwin. We have remained close friends over the years. I have observed her progression from a junior employee to a Doctor of Business, building on her considerable business acumen and commercial accomplishments. Brenda's lived experience is well worth mining to help you build a successful, self-sustaining enterprise.

The Hon Shane L Stone AC KC
www.stonefamilyinaustralia.com.au/family_history/people/
commander-the-honourable-shane-l-stone-ac-pgdk-kc-ran-rtd

PEOPLE: THE MOST IMPORTANT ASPECT OF YOUR BUSINESS

Like most business leaders, you want to do the right thing by your people. You know they are critical to your business success. You do your best to provide a good work environment. You pay competitive salaries and provide industry-standard contracts. You have a morning tea with cake on people's birthdays, and far as you know, all your people get along well. You expect them to work hard and do a good job, and do not exert any undue pressure.

And *now*, with the government introducing new standards focusing on psychosocial safety, you have a requirement to think about all the aspects that could make a difference to their mental health. As a leader in your organisation, sometimes it feels like – well, *what else* is expected of me?

Why these new guidelines?

Details of poor work environments are in the headlines often these days: another sexual harassment claim; evidence of bullying is uncovered; a shortage of psychologists for workplace support;

inappropriate behaviours that continue to be displayed across offices and communication platforms; unreasonable expectations of employees in their jobs; suicide numbers are up in FIFO workers; and high rates of turnover because of interpersonal conflicts or low employee recognition.

It is – now more than ever – challenging to try to structure meaningful and impactful work while ensuring there is inclusiveness and collaboration and still getting the work done on time and to the standard required. You may think this is all becoming too hard. How are you, as a leader, expected to know what is going on when people don't speak up about it until it's too late? It is impossible to watch them all day to ensure they are okay, and you feel if you do, they will claim they are being intimidated by being watched.

The big challenge is that often you think you are doing the right thing by your people and don't know there is a problem because they don't speak up about it. They may tell others at the coffee machine or exchange stories at Friday night drinks, but you may be unaware that anything is wrong. There are so many other things to focus on that sometimes what could be a potential red flag goes under the radar because it hasn't really come your way. The big question is, how are you supposed to know if people don't tell you?

There is a solution that will help you uncover potential problems without watching your people all day, every day, and there is a solution to fix it.

What's *really* going on with your people?

You can find out what is *really* going on by measuring your employee happiness; specifically, the aspects of their workplace that contribute to making them happy – or not. You find out by producing data that will show you how well you and your people are going – how good is that? There is science behind this where you can find the information you need anonymously. This is not just surveying a few of your employees and hoping they have all the information. It is asking *all* of your people and finding out exactly how you and they are doing at each level of the business, and with each leader of the business. How good would it be to be able to write in a tender, under the ever-increasing compliance section, that the measure of your psychosocial safety is at 95% for all areas of the business, and be able to show what you are doing to fill the 5% gap?

Working with leaders of businesses over the past three decades, I have recognised one common theme. Your employees are people, they have similar wants and needs as employees in just about every other business: they want to be heard – as long as it is done confidentially. I started realising this when I was reflecting on the feedback we were receiving on the work we were doing in businesses, which ranged from state and federal government departments to large corporations and includes people who are running their own small to medium businesses. The statements usually contained something like:

- 'All I want is ... '
- 'If I could only ... '
- 'If they would ... '

It was usually about work overload and wanting additional employees, or the new systems not aligning, and significantly a fair bit of missing out on being a parent. This insight was mostly gained when I was working to develop company and project charters with vision and mission statements, underpinned with values. Leading the process to develop the behaviour frameworks provides significant insight not only to what your employees expect of each other, but what is also valuable to them personally.

About me

Much of my work over the past 30 years has been building high-performance teams, both within Australia, across the Pacific and in South East Asia. I enjoy watching the response in workshops when we collaboratively develop a Charter of values and behaviours that align with the business or project's purpose. Hearing the discussions about what the statements mean, how they are applied and what happens if the charter is not adhered to, allows me to understand how well the team will adapt, collaborate and feel empowered. This process is both building a solid foundation for the team members to understand what they are expecting from each other so they effectively work together, as well as building an understanding of what may happen when the values and behaviours are not applied as agreed in the Charter. It is the basis I build my work on in the subsequent professional development sessions, as there is agreement to the framework, and commitment to implement it. Employees want to participate in the workshops as they like to have a say in the behaviours they would like to see in the workplace and what they expect of themselves and others.

In the late 1990s psychosocial safety culture (PSC) was not a phrase that was heard often. There were theories around job demand, resource control and workplace ergonomics, discussions on stress and working nights and weekends – all themes that seemed to me to be related. There was not much dialogue in the workplace at management level around the impact of these work aspects on the employees. I was also doing research at the time on why people were long-term unemployed. I interviewed about 500 people to discover one of the major themes that arose was mental health challenges arising from poor workplace culture, discrimination and bullying, as well as literacy. The research I published in 1999 said that to be successful, business leaders need to *embrace empowerment, devolve decision making and focus on collaborative teamwork*, along with *self-management and people skills*. We use different language a quarter of a century later, however the themes are still the same. The primary theme that emerged is that employees are the most important aspect of our businesses, and many of the leaders didn't seem to recognise this aspect until their important assets depart and they measure the impact of the loss. I have spoken with and interviewed many people on this subject; tested the concepts and analysed the practices in multiple countries, and the themes remain: employees like to work in psychosocially safe work environments where they can feel appreciated, know their work is impactful and that they can collaborate to innovate. This is applicable both in the office and in a hybrid working environment.

My initial research was expanded when I was building a capability framework for the former Queensland lottery business Golden Casket, and then extended across multiple major construction projects and medium-sized companies. During my time at Golden Casket, I received a phone call and was asked if I would like to further my research, which I accepted. Incorporating my theories into my daily work, I proceeded to observe the application of my concepts and conduct research over the following seven years in relation to what makes a happy work environment. When I moved to building high-performance teams for larger infrastructure projects, such as water treatment plants, dams, highways and a rail project, I had a rich source of interactions that I could observe to further understand the impact of how work is organised, what aspects create psychosocial hazards, and the effect of repetitive work and isolation. All of this was done in an environment where we were focusing on merging multiple company cultures concurrently with building fast-track projects. I will admit, it wasn't all smooth sailing, as you will read in some of the examples, however it was a learning experience and allowed me to influence the behaviour in these workplaces, ensuring there were as few psychosocial hazards as possible and that the team members felt happy undertaking impactful work. Recognising I am only one person, the desire to understand the extent that workplaces were happy and psychosocially safe led me to consider building an online platform to measure it. I had collected a significant amount of baseline data, and thinking it would be a waste not to have a way of capitalising on that information so other businesses could also have happy workplaces, the assessment platform became a reality.

If I sound passionate about this work, you bet I am. In my office, I have a token that reminds me why I am so passionate; it is a small square card that was attached to a flower arrangement that was sent to me. The card reads, 'Thank you for saving my life'.

About this book

The Science of Happy Employees will share insights into what you can look for to raise your awareness antenna as to the level of psychosocial safety in your workplace; how happy are your people really feeling? I have included some of the experiences and stories that I have encountered in my work, and some that have been provided to me through interviews. There are stories from government and private sector employees I have interviewed who want to remain anonymous, and there are examples and stories from business owners who are happy for people to know what they are doing to create a safe and happy workplace for their employees.

I discuss what psychosocial safety is, help you understand why it is important, and provide stories to show you the picture of what it really means in your work environment and to your team.

This book is *not a legal volume* that will give you legal advice, case studies or legal precedents, although there are a couple in here for you to ponder. It does give you accounts of what has happened in work environments that I have seen or heard about that contribute to employees feeling unsafe and being unhappy, and to keep it balanced, those who feel safe and happy.

Expect to be taken on a mental rollercoaster, where you may think that the story you are reading couldn't really happen, but unfortunately it did; or where you really would like to see that action happen because it is the culture you would like to build to have happy employees. Read these closely, believe in yourself: you can do it. If you look around, you can see when you have happy employees: you have more productive people who love to work and enjoy what they do. It is your choice; you too can build a culture of happy employees.

As you read you will follow a path of understanding what psychosocial safety is, why it is important and why you need to measure it. By reading the stories of the employees' experiences and understanding the impact their work environment has both on them and your business, you will be able to see how having the right information can create opportunities. These are not only opportunities to be compliant with the Code of Practice – that is a given – but more importantly to have happy, productive employees who love to come to work, who enjoy what they do and can see the contribution they make. Collectively this will ultimately create a more successful and profitable business for you.

That all sounds a bit too easy, doesn't it? And how would I understand the vagaries of your business anyway? Why would people tell *me* how they really feel if they won't tell *you*? Well, I can't answer all of that exactly, however the research and observations I have done across multiple industries have resulted in themes, so I think your business would fit in there.

As for your employees, I can't answer for them individually, however what I will say is that sometimes they do not speak with you because they don't feel safe speaking up, sometimes they don't know who they can speak to, and a lot of times they feel that they will not be believed. It is the sad truth of the hidden world of psychosocial hazards.

You will have seen the word 'science' in the title – that is there for a reason. There is over 17 years of research and testing in here, from within Australia and internationally, identifying and working out what contributes to making happy employees. Now we know we can measure this, and so can you. This base line data comes through my bespoke measuring tool that focuses on the behaviours of your leaders, and how they interact with their employees. It provides the opportunity for your employees to tell how they feel they are treated – the words and behaviours that make the difference, the inclusion or isolation, how much they believe they are appreciated and that their work is impactful. Through the online platform (SHEPS – The **S**cience of **H**appy

Employees Psychosocial Safety), your employees have an opportunity to confidentially assess the frequency of your leaders' and supervisors' behaviours and tell us how safe they feel, what they like about the work environment as well as what is adversely impacting them that needs to be improved. Being invited to participate and feeling heard in a safe environment through an anonymous channel is the proven formula for gaining the truth. Having the truth as a source for action is the most powerful data you will have to build your happy workplace. Isn't that what we all want? To come to work, in our home office, on site or wherever the employee is engaged, find meaning in the work we do and be happy while we do it?

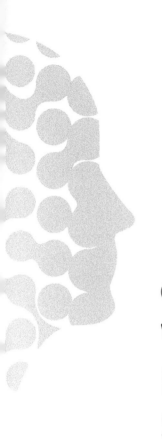

CHAPTER 1
WHAT *IS* PSYCHOSOCIAL SAFETY?

Over 20 years consulting across multiple industries – including major multinational corporations and government departments, education and health, with a specific focus on the infrastructure industry – has provided significant insights into psychosocial safety and psychological wellbeing. Facilitating workshops and conducting health reviews to build positive work environments has shown me that having a psychosocially safe work environment doesn't just happen. It is something you have to work on, consciously and consistently. We all know that we Australians have a propensity to build our personal identity around our job. In fact, it is almost the first thing you learn about people when you meet them. Think about it: when you are at a fundraising dinner for the local football club, cancer research, or an industry awards night, you will be introduced to someone like this: 'This is Cheryl; she is the Project Director of [insert project].' 'Meet Jacob; he is the CFO of [insert company].' It is the same at a barbecue. 'Harry, meet Bill.' 'Hi Bill, what do you do for a living?'

" Given the extent that we focus on our identity attached to our jobs, and remembering we spend close to a third of our prime life years working, why don't we make more of an effort to ensure that the workplace is a happy one?

Given the extent that we focus on our identity attached to our jobs, and remembering we spend close to a third of our prime life years working, why don't we make more of an effort to ensure that the workplace is a happy one? There is a mountain of research – which I won't bother you with – which reinforces that happy workers are more committed and productive workers. I ask you why, then, when we measure and report on other metrics – such as KPIs (key performance indicators), KRIs (key result indicators), OKRs (objectives and key results), LTIFR (lost time injury frequency rate), SSR (site safety rules), SWIMS (safe work method statements) and so on – is PSC (psychosocial safety culture) not at the forefront of our business measures? Why is it that measuring the psychological and social health and wellbeing of our employees – who ensure that we achieve all these other metrics and contribute to the shareholder dividend – is not up there as our number one priority with physical safety?

In a book I authored for the Business Women's Consultative Council on behalf of the Chief Minister of the Northern Territory, I wrote: 'If you think your employees are not your most important asset, try running your business for 30 days without them.' There would not be any metrics to measure in whatever form you choose to measure if you did not have employees to oversee the strategy implementation resulting in the outcomes to measure. Before you start to say that automation and AI are taking over these jobs, yes they are taking over some of the jobs, however there will never in your lifetime or mine be a fully autonomous business. The demand for skilled, psychosocially safe, happy employees will remain for the foreseeable future.

> When I started to talk to people about this book, they'd say to me, 'So, what is psychosocial safety anyway?'

When I started to talk to people about this book, they'd say to me, 'So, what is psychosocial safety anyway?' Really, if you think about it, it's a collection of all those conversations you have with your friends and colleagues – after they have had a bad day listening to employees about flexible work arrangements, requests for extra resources and support, and outcomes that are yet to be achieved that have missed deadlines. Reflecting on the week, you realise it was filled with formal meetings and spontaneous meetings with employees. The dialogue focused around work priorities and possible overload, with supervisors feeling that they continually have to tell employees what to do and how to do it. Additionally, people were being held accountable for something they didn't even know was their job. All these factors contribute to your colleague spoiling your after-work relaxing red wine or scotch on ice because they are having a bad day yet again. They are describing to you what is not a psychosocially safe workplace. The high stress levels and the focus on aspects where employees need to perform their best indicate that all is not as it should be in that business.

I'd like to share with you what happens in the work environment when there is *not* appropriate psychosocial safety. Following are insights from an international student studying her Masters in International Business. She was attending one of my Monday lectures, and having arrived early we started chatting about how we spent the weekend. My discussion was focused on the interviews I had been doing of people who were in psychosocial unsafe workplaces, to which Sharon replied that she knew exactly what I was talking about. She, like many, had taken a position as a support worker with a large national aged-care facility to earn money while she was studying. I asked if I could interview her on her experiences; she agreed provided I did not personally identify her. We agreed to call her Sharon, and this is her story of working in an environment in late 2023 that was not psychosocially safe.

Sharon was employed to assist with mealtimes for the elderly residents of the aged-care facility. The role involved a shift from seven in the morning until two, with a change over for the afternoon shift from two to seven. Sharon tells me that, although there was a job description, systems, procedures and processes to follow, they were not formalised and she could never do her job to the required standard because of the supervisor's rotating shift rosters:

> Everyone wants it their way, and every day there is someone changing something for no reason that I can see except it makes them feel in charge. And the next time somebody comes for a check up, they will add to the workload by saying, 'Oh, have you done this?', which isn't your job but because there is always a shortage of nurses someone has to do it so it is given to us.

I questioned her: is it about preferences, or is it workload and the effective use of time? She responded:

> Sometimes you won't even have time to take a break before the chef from another location, like the head office, arrives and adds something more to what needs to be done today. At times the nurses will also delegate their tasks to you, as the management doesn't want to pay extra. I hadn't been paid for a shift I worked until eight o'clock. Several staff members resigned because of this payment issue, leading to the recruitment of new personnel.

I questioned if she tried to talk with management about it.

> Actually, I quickly found another job and then I just resigned. You should be motivated and the manager should listen to the staff. They have high turnover, and it is costing them a lot.

Unfortunately Sharon's story is not an isolated case: the lack of role clarity and standard operating procedures, resource shortages, bullying, and the inability to surface concerns without repercussions created not only a sense of anxiety and fear of going into the work environment, it also did not allow her to work at her best. Sharon is also correct it is costing her former employer a lot; both in financial costs as well as reputational costs.

I was explaining these issues to a colleague of mine who is a senior partner in a moderate-size accounting firm that has multiple geographically displaced offices. He responded, 'And now we have to be responsible for their mental health?' You know it is highly unlikely you will have one of your Senior Accountants, or any of your employees for that matter, storm into your office and say, 'We need to talk because I don't feel psychosocially safe.' And he is correct. Tackling psychosocial safety is about understanding the workplace and setting a culture where there is a genuine preparedness to listen and to act on what has been heard. You will have discussions that include the words 'stress', 'overload', 'insufficient resources', claims of 'harassment', and similar. These keywords are flagging to you the psychological health of your employees.

The image opposite shows how stress can affect your people and suggests some of the behaviours you may observe that are flags your staff are stressed and the workplace is developing an unsafe culture of unacceptable expectations.

The fact is you as an employer or business leader have always had a duty of care to provide a safe work environment, including psychological and social aspects. The difference now is the increased awareness through the legislated Code of Practice. Reflect on this: you made an effort some years ago to introduce cross-cultural training, then ensured bullying awareness

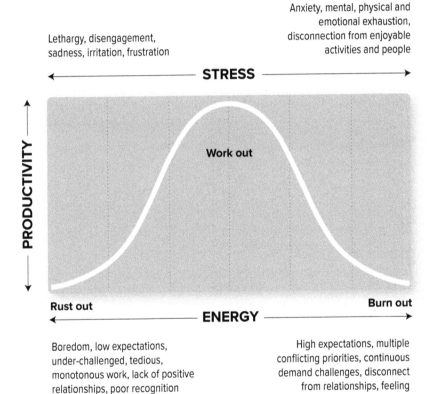

Anxiety, mental, physical and emotional exhaustion, disconnection from enjoyable activities and people

Lethargy, disengagement, sadness, irritation, frustration

STRESS

PRODUCTIVITY

Work out

Rust out

Burn out

ENERGY

Boredom, low expectations, under-challenged, tedious, monotonous work, lack of positive relationships, poor recognition or appreciation

High expectations, multiple conflicting priorities, continuous demand challenges, disconnect from relationships, feeling under-appreciated training was delivered each year or so, and more recently, diversity and inclusion training. All of this contributes to a safe workplace, showing that you are taking positive steps to minimise psychosocial hazards and mitigate potential risks. The question is, how well are you doing this, and is it enough? Awareness of the responsibility to provide a psychosocially safe work environment was low because it wasn't given a title. We have a tendency to label behaviours and attach them to legislation and policy, aiming to increase awareness and compliance. Psychosocial safety is the next label that you are integrating into the way you do business.

With the Code of Practice (which has different names in different states) now being incorporated under the state equivalent of the Work Health and Safety Act, realisation of the importance of psychosocial health has increased. This simply means being aware of the circumstances within the work environment that could contribute to promoting positive wellbeing and being aware of what may be around the office that could be considered a hazard to the psychological and social aspects of work. Now I hear you saying that is a bit hard given the extent of diversity in your employees; some work from home, others are in an office and some are simply having fun that others take offence to, and how are you expected to predict that? Awareness of the Code of Practice is a good start. The next step is perhaps measuring psychosocial safety in your company as this will give you an understanding of how well the Code of Practice is being applied and where the gaps are.

“ In a nutshell, psychosocial safety is keeping the workplace free from anything that could cause harm to your employees' psychological and workplace social health.

In a nutshell, psychosocial safety is keeping the workplace free from anything that could cause harm to your employees' psychological and workplace social health. But there are so many different expectations from each of your team members – how can you identify it all or keep up with it? The truth is, you don't know what you don't know, so I encourage you to find out. The first step to finding out is building your awareness.

Building your awareness of psychosocial safety

To help you start to build your awareness I will share a couple of examples from my experience that will provide insight. It is important that you recognise you can't know it all or action what you think needs doing all at once. You do, however, have comfort knowing there is a scientific way of finding out where you are now on the Psychosocial Safety Culture scale and what to do to ensure you have a safe and happy workplace where your employees love to come to work.

Firstly, let's consider awareness. Awareness is an interesting phenomenon and can best be explained by saying it is when you know or remember something, but it may not be at the forefront of your consciousness. A simple way to illustrate this is when you're asked a joke you know you've heard before, like the ones in last year's Christmas bonbon. They're typically simple, non-offensive, and a bit quirky, such as, 'Why did the biscuit go to the doctor? Because its world was crumbling.' If you're asked that joke in January, you might remember it because you heard it several times at Christmas lunches the previous month. But if you're asked it at a Christmas in July party, you're likely to respond with, 'I know that one, but I can't remember the answer.' There is a level of awareness that you find difficult to recall when put on the spot to answer.

How about a different kind of awareness? Let's say you're considering replacing your current LandCruiser because you no longer need that type of vehicle and the lease is coming to an end. While waiting at the traffic lights over the weekend, you spotted a Mercedes AMG Black Metallic SUV in the showroom on the corner. You could envision yourself driving it to the coast for holidays with the family. You placed an order for it, thinking you'd have a unique car, only to suddenly realise there are many of these AMGs already on the road, and most of them are black. This is awareness working at its fullest. Once something has been brought to your attention, your heightened awareness will be alert for it, if you choose it to be there.

This concept also applies to the awareness of the environment you work in; the extent that people are having fun or not, the way there is effective collaboration or not, and how balanced the workloads are ... or not. This is awareness of psychosocial safety; it is knowing the keys or triggers to look and listen for and to be alert to. Think about this conversation that I was an adjunct to. I was on a consulting project within a government-owned corporation, waiting to speak with Jamie the Project Director. He was concluding a conversation with Lorraine, and I heard him say, 'So the work schedule is agreed.' Lorraine, standing there with an arm full of documents and an iPad, responded with a single word – 'Yes.' Jamie went on: 'We understand timelines will be tight and there will be late nights because I don't have anyone else available, but I am sure you can get it done by Monday lunchtime as that gives you three solid days and the weekend if you need. I know you can do it.' The same single word *yes* was muttered by Lorraine, and she turned to pack her files into her carry bag. Just as I was about to open my mouth to speak to Jamie he swung his chair around and said to Lorraine in a very casual way: 'By the way, there is a half-day session tomorrow looking at the potential changes to the planning statements. They need our discipline input and I am too snowed under so I said you were as good as me with this stuff and that you would be there. It is on the fifth floor and it starts at 9.00 am.' I don't know Lorraine's response – I didn't hear her say anything, however I did feel that there was a change in the level of tension. As Lorraine walked off and Jamie gave me his attention, he said to me, 'It's okay, Lorraine is a great team player.' In effect, Jamie had recognised that Lorraine was overloaded with work, had a critical deadline, and yet he went on to commit more for her to try to fit into her schedule. I am unsure if this was a one-off occurrence or a habit of Jamie's leadership.

What do you think of this behaviour? There are multiple ways to look at this. The first being, is this Jamie's natural leadership style? If so, it appears he doesn't have a concept of how constant high work demands with intense concentration and pressure over time can contribute to poor mental wellbeing. If it is a habit it could collectively create a risk of harm due to Lorraine's continual work overload, low support and inability to access sufficient resources. If Lorraine can't talk with him about it (and it didn't seem like she could), this inevitably could sink into a poor working relationship and eventually an outcome that nobody would like to see. The outcomes could include stress leave and a possible workers compensation claim, or if Lorraine stepped outside her personal fear and reluctance and tried to speak up in an unsafe environment, the loss of a valuable resource as a result of Lorraine leaving. Given that Jamie had identified a lack of resources and appears to rely on Lorraine, I am sure he really doesn't want any of those to eventuate.

What else happens in a psychosocially safe workplace? Well, it's about balancing the amount of control your employees have over their jobs. Now, the technical term for this is 'self-determination'. How much control an individual can exert over their job tasks is a significant consideration. It revolves around the comprehension that certain desired outcomes must be achieved, within a predetermined timeline, and the capability of the employee to influence the realisation of those outcomes. For example, it's not a requirement to adhere strictly to a predetermined schedule outlined by someone else for every moment of the workday, but it may be a requirement that specific tasks and outcomes be achieved. There exists a level of autonomy where the individual holds sway. This may be with a bookkeeper who understands the compliance requirements both within the company and legislatively and who can plan their own day based on energy levels and ability to focus to ensure that all is completed. Understanding the extent of control one employs within their job becomes crucial. There are two aspects to this: role clarity and empowerment. Let's talk about role clarity first.

Understanding role clarity

Role clarity is more than telling a new person on their first day what is expected of the job. Do they really know what their role is? Oh, yes, there are the position descriptions; all roles will have, or at least should have, a position description. But there's a big difference between what's written down on a piece of paper designed for recruitment and what your employees actually do on the job.

Here's a challenge:

- Look at today's date, and now think about your job title and description. Are they the same as this time last year?

- Now think about what you have focused on in the past three months; what have been your achievements and challenges? Are they the same as this time last year?

- Now look at your job description; how much of what you have focused on and achieved over the past three months is actually detailed in your position description?

When I ask this question in face-to-face discussions, I inevitably get a yes to the first question and no as an answer for the second question and a wow for the last. This is the nature of business: the need to adapt to emerging circumstances and industry requirements, adopt new processes and procedures, and apply a different strategic lens due to multiple forces such as global trends and client demands. Role clarity is therefore a case of understanding the role quadrant, the difference between role, responsibility, authority and accountability; or as I refer to it, your 'RRAA quadrant'.

For your employees to have a hazard-free RRAA, it needs to be in balance. Think of the four letters RRAA as representing one each of the four legs of the table you were sitting at to drink your coffee this morning. Were the legs balanced and the table stable, so when you put your coffee down you felt comfortable it would not topple over and spill everywhere? The same is true for your employees' roles. They need to understand **role** – that is, the name of what they are doing, such as Director of Marketing; and **responsibilities** – the aspects they are responsible for. This is usually clear, and most employees understand this.

What is not usually clear and can contribute to anxiety and stress is the correct alignment of **authority** and **accountability**. Authority is often seen in the delegation matrix and usually relates to financial delegations, and accountability is usually associated with ensuring the delegations are not transgressed. Where does the rest of the responsibility and accountability for employee wellbeing reside, and how is it communicated? An example comes from a senior public servant. He works for a government-owned corporation. These organisations have two competing masters; they try to make money for the government by providing a service and are subjected to the public sector compliance and regulation frameworks. Positions in these types of entities can at best be described as bureaucratically challenging. I asked him how he was enjoying his new role. He told me he was straddling two roles, as the new one had some strategic objectives that needed to be delivered at a clipping pace. But there were two primary challenges:

- He hadn't been relieved of his responsibilities for delivering the outcomes on his past role, and
- Although there were expectations to deliver in the new role, the resources to deliver were not being made available.
  He said, 'The sign-off decision-making delegation is so slow, I can't move on quotes to get the progress that is needed.'

This means he has clarity on his role and responsibility. He knows what needs to be done by when, and how, but he doesn't have the authority to make the decisions for which he will be held accountable if not delivered on time. His coffee table is certainly out of balance, with psychosocial health hazards readily spilling onto the floor, such as lack of delegation and resources, work overload and poor senior support to achieve the predetermined outcomes. Who will take the accountability if the outcomes are not achieved and who will take the glory if they are? The sad fact is, in a psychosocially unsafe workplace the person accountable and the person taking the glory will be different people – and they should not be.

I will challenge you to think – do you and your senior leaders know where their RRAA sits within the realm of psychosocial safety? When I ask this question of key leaders, I usually get one of three responses:

- Firstly, 'We have a great culture here and we all have each other's backs.'
- Sometimes it is, 'We have a People and Culture division and they look after that.'
- And the third and most disheartening response, 'Oh yes, we have to look after that now also ... but how are we expected to know?' You can know by making the effort to find out.

That is the first aspect of role clarity. Now let's look at the much talked about aspect of job control: empowerment.

Understanding empowerment

Empowerment is a word that is used a lot in human resources circles, however it is the action of the leaders that will demonstrate if your employees actually feel empowered or not. The SHEPS survey explores five aspects of empowerment. It asks you to consider if your leaders are applying these principles with their team members:

- encouraging employees to take initiative, make decisions, and follow through on them
- building self-efficacy and confidence in others
- providing meaningful challenges that promote growth
- developing trust and inspiring others
- offering effective coaching and feedback
- facilitating input and participation from employees.

Now, they all look like good statements by themselves. However, when your employees feel that they can go about their work and get it done the best way they know how, and check in with their leader when they need support, it provides a great sense of self-satisfaction and self-worth. Both are aspects of developing a happy employee, and have a positive impact in your business. When employees know that they can make a decision and their leader will be there to listen, challenge, and even back them, that builds trust and inspires the employees to want to give more. Your employees do not wake up and decide they want a boring day, where they want to be told what to do and how to do it; this is what AI and automation are for. Coaching your employees to be thinkers, decision makers, and to lead themselves in doing the best job means that trust and empowerment are in action. This results in an increased level of happiness, higher quality work, and an increased profitability score on the finance report. Let me show you how this works.

One of the national businesses I was working with, which I will not name, decided they did want to find out how happy their employees were. This business has offices in all states of Australia and employees working in multiple areas across the more heavily populated eastern coast. They are heavily focused on providing workplace training and safety advice, and like a lot of service businesses they provide this under a combined pay-as-you-go and annual subscription model; an approach that requires significant investment in customer service. The business has a structured approach to and readily invests in employee development. I was approached to conduct an assessment of the level of psychosocial safety in the work environment. The request was prompted because the board believed there was not sufficient measurement of the leadership's effectiveness, nor any baseline on the extent to which the business was psychosocially safe.

They saw the value in understanding the metrics and wanted to benchmark where the business sat currently, and to see what – if anything – needed to be done to ensure they were building the best possible culture for their employees. Like all surveys, the link to the questionnaire is sent by email, and on the bottom of the email it advises the participant to please contact me if they have any concerns or questions, and I include an email and phone number. The agreement was made and the emails were sent to the leaders and employees to assess the company, there was no real pressing concern, more a company setting its safety baseline. As it eventuated the biggest concern from the employees was seeking a reinforcement of the guarantee of confidentiality, because 'one of the key leaders [was] acting in a passive aggressive way and using his position and role as a way to mask his inappropriate behaviour'. Further discussion revealed that this leader was head of People and Culture, who had told the employees that he would read all responses because he needed to know what was going on in the company. The concern from the team was so deep that I offered to conduct online video information forums and also had individual question-and-answer sessions to allay the fear that was being expressed by his words and behaviour. Following reassurances to the employees that they could complete the questionnaire honestly as I was the only one who would see the answers, most of them went ahead and completed the survey. The employees felt they had to gain confidence that the head of People and Culture would not get any insight into who said what specifically. This pre-survey dialogue indicated loudly and clearly to me that there were some psychosocial hazards in the work environment and that possibly some of those risks were located in the People and Culture team.

Based on these pre-survey interactions, it would appear there was a lack of trust between the head of People and Culture and the employees. Such was the depth of the mistrust, the employees couldn't follow the business's safety in the workplace policy and go to his office as a safe place to discuss their lack of psychosocial wellbeing. The hazards were going unreported, or if they were reported, they were dismissed as not carrying credibility. It is these indicators that may or may not be heard or observed by other people that are addressed in the questions in the survey, as it is designed to provide indicators that there is a challenge needing to be addressed and where the challenge is stemming from. The results of that particular survey gave insight into not only the presence of psychosocial hazards in the business, it showed clearly they were stemming from a place that was supposed to be the safe place and where the responsibility for identifying hazards was held.

Why wasn't the challenge addressed sooner? Sometimes the presence of interpersonal fear draws a mask across the hazard and others in the business don't know. The leaders are unaware of some of the covert behaviour being applied and it is not reported to the leadership team meetings because it is not being reported through the correct channel because the channel is unsafe, therefore the vortex continues unabated. In this case where the board thought was the safe place was not actually a safe place. The hazards were being held undercover through fear. This company is not an isolated case, and the extent of unsafe practices has been evidenced in the Australian media recently.

Being alert to bullying and harassment

On the front page of the *Courier Mail*, a newspaper published in Queensland Australia, on Saturday 14 October 2023 the headline shouted in bold print 'Water Torture'. The article, written by Julian Linden, reported on the findings of an independent report on the 'toxic culture' of the Australian women's swimming team who 'were subject to physical and mental abuse, groping, disgusting sexual innuendo, body shaming and public humiliation'. A week prior to this, in the *Australian Financial Review* on the weekend of 7–8 October 2023, another article was headlined 'Revamp Over "Sexism Racism and Bullying"', about the report from an independent investigation of the Productivity Commission where the 'investigation uncovered a culture of harassment, bullying, discrimination and victimisation'. And unfortunately an article published by ABC news on 28 December 2023 about the workplace culture of the Australian Arctic Division's 'predatory culture' reported that '30 percent [said] that it was easier to keep quiet'.

> Unfortunately, harassment and bullying are still rife in the workplace.

The sad aspect of these reports is that the organisations required independent investigations to enable a sufficiently safe environment for the employees being harassed and bullied to share their experiences without fear or judgment, and without pressure to sugar-coat or understate their poor treatment and the practices that were making their workplace psychologically and psychosocially unsafe. Unfortunately, harassment and bullying are still rife in the workplace. Yes, these unacceptable practices are still there, and some of the major workplace hazards that make it unsafe don't really take that much to fix – to remove the hazard and to manage the risk.

In this book I will show you what this means and how you can actually measure whether your people are happy. You can measure whether they feel they have your support, and you can collect some scientific data to show if they feel safe working with their leaders and in their current circumstances. And what does that mean? It means that when you know, and your employees know, you are trying to make workplace improvements and a better work environment, it creates a safer environment by default. Your employees see that you are trying, and you are working to develop a culture of safety and trust where they can feel comfortable to tell you if you are making improvements in the right areas, and not 'finding it easier to keep quiet'. Actual behaviours are not scientific, but being able to know where the adjustments in the behaviours – and where specifically in a work environment – are required is critical to managing hazards. Getting this right means you *can* build a safe, positive culture and have happy employees. That's what you can measure. And when you have access to the tools to measure it, you know what to target for improvement. Knowing what to target means you can change just a few behaviours to have a major impact resulting in a happier work environment. You don't have to change every behaviour and everything. You will know from the results specifically what to focus on and where, impacting positively on the leaders' behaviours and subsequently the whole environment. When you specifically target and impact a few of the right behaviours you create a ripple effect and they have an influence on others, resulting in a significant compounding improvement. Measuring means you have the science underneath to illustrate what you have done and how you have done it; remeasuring shows you the impact of your interventions and the ripple effect it has. This means you know your employees work because they want to because they love what they do and they are happy to do it, with an absence of fear, knowing they can speak out without reprisal, knowing they will be heard. Setting up a positive environment such as this allows employees to feel they are appreciated. Appreciation is a motivating factor for employees to make an extra effort in the work that they do.

Managing rewards and recognition

When your employees have a safe work environment that allows them to be happy, they can perform at their best, and they often like to celebrate this. The best way to celebrate is with rewards and recognition.

Leaders I have worked with in both the public and private sectors have awards that recognise individuals for their outstanding effort or contribution to something that made a significant difference to the department or one of the department stakeholders. The recipients value the recognition because it demonstrates they are being seen, heard and publicly acknowledged, by their peers who nominated them and their leaders who supported them. It's a personal value attached to the recognition. It is a public thank you.

> Some employees need recognition and some people just get on with it.

Recognition is really hard to get right, for multiple reasons. Large corporations and the public sector have to stick to the pay levels and scales set for them, and awards and agreements that are determined by the workplace agreements. Let me assure you there are two aspects of this: both reward *and* recognition. Some employees need recognition and some people just get on with it. Deep down, recognition is a more powerful motivator than reward and everybody likes to be appreciated; it is the public acknowledgement that is the compounding factor. It is recognising and understanding that your employees are the key to value-adding to your business, to fostering innovation and achieving your strategy, because it is your employees who transform your strategy into reality. There are some who shy away from such celebrations and do not feel motivated by the public recognition, privately however most of them crave it as a means of justification to themselves. These employees often express that they prefer to work alone. They don't quite say these words, however they are the ones who put their hands up and volunteer when there are projects that don't require a team effort.

Putting loneliness on your radar

Humans naturally are social beings; some like to be more social than others. However, loneliness is one of the psychosocial safety hazards that tends to be overlooked. With increased hybrid working arrangements and flexibility in where work is conducted, loneliness as a psychosocial hazard can easily slip under your radar. Ending Loneliness Together is Australia's national organisation working to raise awareness and reduce the negative effects of chronic loneliness and social isolation in our communities through evidence-based interventions and advocacy. In their report 'State of the Nation Report: Social Connection in Australia 2023', they remind us of the important distinction between social isolation and loneliness. They write:

> while many Australians believe they [social isolation and loneliness] are one and the same, there is a significant difference. Loneliness is a distressing feeling we get when we feel disconnected from other people, and desire more (or more

satisfying) social relationships. Social isolation (or being alone) is a physical state where you have fewer interactions with others.

This tells us you can have employees working in your business who are physically present and are still experiencing loneliness. This is the case for Heidi. The daughter of immigrants, Heidi went to a private girls' school where she felt out of place and failed to develop close friendships with any of the other students. This left her devoid of the social skills that teenage girls develop. Heidi went on to work in what she described as 'backroom jobs' – those that required high levels of interaction with computers and little interaction with people. Her level of interaction was so low she did not take breaks and ate her lunch at her desk, taking only half of the allocated hour for her lunch break, and she left work half an hour early to avoid the rush on the train. When I asked her if she felt lonely in her self-imposed social isolation her response was that 'no one cared to ask anyway so what difference did it make?' The challenge with Heidi is that one situation seemed to morph into the other until she had a self-perpetuating internal isolation maelstrom. Her behaviour looked positive because she worked hard and took on the work of others when they went for professional development sessions, a great avoidance tactic. This resulted in her becoming unemployable because her skills became redundant. The jobs, mainly data entry, were replaced by AI and her social network to contact former colleagues seeking employment was nonexistent. A sad but true case of isolation in the workplace not being actively noticed or managed.

Isolation is one aspect that can flag a hazard challenge – the departure of good and competent staff is potentially more than a flag, it is an alarm bell. Let's however not be alarmist and we will call it a flag.

> " One of the flags to be aware of is when a good,
> competent and valuable team member resigns.

One of the flags to be aware of is when a good, competent and valuable team member resigns. A leader with poor psychosocial safety awareness is likely to believe that if they give the team member a pay rise they should be happy and choose to stay in their job. This doesn't work. It may be effective in the short term, but it's not a long-term strategy. There is a reason the person made their decision to leave. Money is not a motivator to stay in the work environment. Much more important are the levels of leadership satisfaction, safety and the empowerment they feel, and their ability to be adaptable and to collaborate in their role. These are some of the aspects which if presented at acceptable levels would have prevented the resignation. Not money. The employee may stay for a short period with extra money, however they have mentally left and therefore the level of happiness will not be there. They will leave and often it is within a period of 12 months of the initial resignation.

When I ask if there are exit interviews, it is often a tick-the-box exercise because the person conducting the interview feels embarrassed that there wasn't a way to retain the team member and often the person is conveniently unavailable due to handover demands. Not being available is an avoidance strategy. The better approach is to have an independent consultant undertake the exit interview, away from the work environment. The purpose is to understand the challenges of and drivers for the employee's resignation and to wish them the best in their move. This is a valuable approach, however the value is only realised if there is action taken. It is up to you to ensure you act on the feedback.

You may be surprised what you discover. The importance of the independent exit interview is twofold:

- Firstly, the independence will increase the likelihood of the exiting employee truthfully sharing the reasons that contributed to the resignation, rather than the coding that we often hear such as wanting to spend more time with the family or feeling the need for a sea change or tree change.
- Secondly, it provides information to act on. As an independent does not have insight as to how your business fully operates, they will ask the probing questions that an internal person won't as they attach assumptions to the answers. As a result of this process you now have valuable information – the people who leave are a goldmine, however the value of that gold mined by the independent interviewer will only be realised when it is acknowledged and acted on in a proactive and positive way.

Due to employee turnover I was engaged by the chairman of a tourism business to review the leadership approach of the executive of one of their multiple businesses. The agreed approach was to initially undertake some observations and, if necessary, have a few informal conversations with the team to see what they thought the leaders were doing well and what could be done to improve the way the work was organised and other work-related factors. Undertaking this consultancy was somewhat of a surprising journey. The duplicity uncovered in the leadership interactions within and across the teams compared with what was written in the monthly board reports was nothing short of astounding. The leaders had what we call an 'anchoring' bias. They appeared to be biased towards those team members they had been involved in hiring and biased against those who were hired without their involvement. This created a fragmented culture where everyone was watching their step, to see if they were 'in the in or out group this week'.

The leaders were relying on the first piece of information that they were given in relation to the behaviour of a team member: it might be a small complaint from one of the customers or a team member; it might be that they assisted another team member outside their designated role, such as making the coffee rather than managing the till payments; or they failed to sufficiently upsell in the retail area. Once this was brought to the attention of the leader, if it was one of the staff they were not involved with recruiting, the leader would seek out additional information to support that the employee was not doing what the leader thought they should be doing. They actively sought proof that this apparently one-off inappropriate act was potentially a repeated behaviour. The leaders actively looked for things to reinforce the conclusion they had come to based on their natural bias against the person, and not necessarily the facts of the situation. The employees therefore constantly felt they had to be alert as to the presence of the leaders in case they said or did something the leader did not approve of; not the happiest environment to work in when the leaders were operating on a basis of anchoring bias. Anchoring bias can be used for good or for bad, and these leaders were not using their bias for the good of the employees they had chosen for personal reasons to dislike. Bias when used for good is usually anchored to standards about product quality and/or customer service.

When used for good, you can imagine the entire team will thank you for this. Roz White, a well-known community-focused director of multiple family-owned companies on the Sunshine Coast – including six IGA stores – with approximately 500 employees, uses bias for good from a standards perspective combined with capitalising on what her employees bring. She openly admits that she is 'unapologetic about having high standards' and the foundation of her business success is in 'retaining professional respect through integrity and living the values. The employees who embrace the boundaries, policies and are willing to grow socially and environmentally with a duty of care to others have a high degree of satisfaction and accomplishment because they love to develop and flourish. A small number fall away during the journey and you know that they are not fit for the business and that is okay.' Anchoring bias when used from a negative perspective is harmful to both the employees and the business; it is a potential hazard. When done from a positive position, professional respect through integrity and living the values is evident, and the employees benefit. Consider your anchoring biases. How are they affecting your employees?

> We know from experience and from research that 99 happy employees are more productive employees.

This is the recognition and understanding that we all make mistakes and can learn from them; it is creating a no-blame culture. It is not and should not be about punishment. Your employees might not openly thank you for it. You won't receive thank you cards or a bottle of your favourite beverage, however the gratitude will be reflected in the productivity, output and the achievement of goals by happier employees. We know from experience and from research that happy employees are more productive employees.

Managing diversity

In recent years, we've witnessed a surge in the levels of anxiety experienced by our workforce. The challenge lies in balancing diversity in the workplace; the diversity of locations, hybrid work from anywhere or working from home, open acceptance of sexual identity diversity, and significant ethnic and cultural diversity. Certain words and behaviours that are accepted within one cultural social group might not be accepted by other culturally diverse employees. When we attempt to overlay an organisational culture that embraces diversity, the challenge arises: how do we find the balance? How can we ensure negative workplace conflict doesn't occur and it doesn't spiral into an unsafe workplace because there are employees who were born in countries that are now opposing each other or are at war?

The critical part is firstly to recognise that this may occur, and the second is to manage it through obtaining a valid measurement to baseline. This can be achieved through SHEPS, my assessment tool that will allow you to understand if there are any hazards, and if there are, where the hazards are stemming from. SHEPS is an abbreviation for the Science of Happy Employees Psychosocial Safety. It is a valuable and confidential process, with reassurance for participants they will not be identified. It is the leaders who will be identified through the feedback reports. Through this process we can start to find the root cause of what's behind feelings of unease, lack of productivity and the unhappiness of employees. Identification is the first stage, and what the identification does is allow you to invest in a solution that is going to work, not what you think is going to work. (We will look at SHEPS in more detail later.)

Recognising fear

Finding the people who don't like to work in your organisation is another way of finding gold, as these are often the people who contribute to creating the adverse social factors in your workplace.

It's not about ignoring them or putting them under a performance management plan. It's about understanding why they do not like to work in your business, and then understanding what is contributing to the business being like that. Employment is after all a two-way process. When you understand why your business has undesirable attributes you will be able to do something about it. And yes, there will be people who will not want to tell you, no matter what approach you use. There may be people who have mental health challenges who may be highly anxious and want to hide, however usually the only reason they hide and fail to mention it is fear. It might be a fear of losing their job. It might be a fear of repercussions from a particular leader or treatment from team members, or fear carried over from previous workplace experiences. Fear is a byproduct of a culture built on inappropriate leadership, poor application of values and an unsafe culture that is not focused on prioritising employees as the most vital ingredient in business success. It is important to make sure that any fear is acknowledged and that the acknowledgement comes from a genuine empathetic place.

What is crucial is understanding the underlying factors driving the fear and establishing a workplace environment where employees feel empowered to contribute without fear. It is important to eliminate, as much as possible, the fear of inadvertently saying something wrong, which could lead to humiliation or reprisals. Employees with high levels of anxiety will often carry the fear of saying something wrong and the fear of being judged because of their contribution. Anxiety is their internal conflict of this fear and prior to a meeting they will often carry the fear of being asked a question, which to them is a known danger point. They will be equally fearful of not responding to an assumed expected standard, which may contribute to raising their anxiety because they believe they should know the required response and perhaps don't. Building an inclusive nonjudgmental environment where robust conversations can be had is essential to building a happy work environment. Building such an environment, however, will require time, and the journey is longer for some employees than others. I encourage you to start somewhere. You won't be perfect, but slowly, as you come to understand the scientific basis of the culture that is driven by the behaviours in your business and understand how it can be measured and what can be done to improve it, you will be on the right path. Your journey then becomes one of an upward spiral of progress through measurement of identification, implementation, reflection, learning, adjustment and remeasurement. This will be explained in more depth later in the book, however what is important to understand here, and you will notice in the diagram opposite, is that as you implement, reflect and adjust, the breadth of the hazards diminishes.

Despite all the attention in the media on suicides, mental health and wellbeing, the exponential increase in mental health challenges being experienced by our colleagues and members of our communities is phenomenal. According to an article dated 2 November 2022 on the Australian Government website Job Access, a failure to adequately respond to the needs of employees suffering mental health challenges is costing Australian businesses $11 billion a year.[1] That is not a typo. It really says $11,000,000,000.

---

1   www.jobaccess.gov.au/news-media/mental-health-inaction-costing-businesses-11bn-annually.

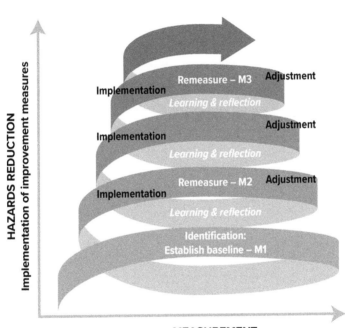

" Leaders must aim to ensure that team members come to work because they genuinely want to, driven by a sense of safety and the opportunity to make a meaningful difference.

Employers have an opportunity to help to counterbalance the extraordinary costs. Leaders must aim to ensure that team members come to work because they genuinely want to, driven by a sense of safety and the opportunity to make a meaningful difference. Creating an environment conducive to your employees' motivation is key to fostering their desire to be at work. This was evidenced on a fast-track civil and structural construction project I was working on, where my role was to build a high-performance team. It was a joint venture involving workers from five different companies who all had their jobs and all knew what was expected of them. I noticed changed behaviour from one of the female engineers: she would ensure that she was not in the lunchroom alone, she would walk the long way back to her workstation, and she became reserved. Although it took some time to have her share reasons behind the observed changes, we were able to establish that she was being subjected to sexual harassment by another person on the project. This man worked for her company, claimed strong family and religious commitments, and was senior in role to her both in the company and on the project. She thought that because the harassment occurred when nobody else was able to observe it, she would not be believed and her role on the project would be terminated, because he was more senior and therefore considered more valuable. On that project we didn't have a method for her to report anonymously, however we did have a reporting process and she did report it, and the investigation was completed thoroughly in a confidential way. The male engineer did not return to the project after a weekend home with his family. There was a lot of work involved in this, first and foremost for the female engineer to understand that she would be believed and protected, as well as a full investigation being carried out. Discreetness in the investigation was paramount and appropriate action essential. Vital to this process was for the employees to understand that no person is more important than others and inappropriate behaviours will not be tolerated. This was a true reflection of the comment in the address at the International Women's Day Conference (2013) by the then Chief of the Australian Army, Lieutenant General David Morrison, 'The standard you walk past is the standard you accept.'

Although there was a high level of discretion and the case was not spoken about in the management team meetings, the appreciation was overheard in the lunchroom discussions with statements like, 'I am pleased he didn't come back from leave; he always made me feel uncomfortable,' and, 'It's great he is not here; now I don't have to worry if I have to work late and he is the only one here.' None of this was evident until after he had left. In this case the absence was felt in a positive way. It also illustrates the power of observation and being willing to ask if you believe that someone's behaviour is changing for no evident reason. The subtleties can speak loudly if you will listen.

Acknowledging all contributors

One of the challenges I often notice is the failure to recognise the equal contribution everybody makes. I was working with a construction team around 2020; we were about to go to site on a very significant project, and I asked them who the most important person was on the project. This was not really an exercise in who was the most important, more a process in understanding and recognising the value that each and every person on the job made, and that every role no matter the title makes a significant contribution to the success of the project. The project's total worth was about a billion dollars. We had engineers, project directors, project managers, stakeholder communications people, and many more. There was a group of about 50 people, and I asked them, 'Who is going to be the most important person on this project?' When the project is that big, each person looked at their role and how it connected with the others around the room, and they collectively agreed that everyone in the room contributed significantly to the project. I prompted them to reconsider their perspective and urged them to consider those who would be involved in the project who weren't present. Responses centred on individuals such as those working in the field, traffic controllers and plant operators. While this extended their thinking to another tier, it remained primarily focused on the immediate task at hand.

From there I suggested they consider whether Peggy (the cleaner) was the most important person on the project. Why? Because I know from experience that this is a very crucial role, and often it is not given the equal respect to the positions of Project Manager or Senior Engineer. It has been demonstrated that when the workers come in for lunch and it's hot and humid they expect the air conditioner in the mess hut to be working, however sometimes it is not working because no one's asked for it to be seen to. Then the microwave is not clean, and they can't heat their food, or there are no forks for them to eat their lunch. What happens? The workers get grumpy. When they become grumpy, their focus shifts from the job to the problem at hand. This heightened focus on the issue increases the chances of accidents on site. Additionally, it reduces team productivity as members might not have had the chance to cool down, eat adequately, or enjoy their break. Rushing through lunch leaves them dissatisfied, impacting their subsequent work.

I think the message here is clear. The challenge is to understand the compounding impact in the service chain, to recognise and celebrate everybody has a critical role and understand how that critical role impacts on everyone else's physical, social and mental wellbeing. This is an illustration of how psychosocial safety is not a standalone process; it has compounding impacts dependant on employees' actions or inactions and should be a critical aspect of your business processes and particularly in understanding the impact that each part of the system has on each of the other parts of the system.

> By fostering mutual respect, an environment of trust develops.

A key therefore to happy employees is to understand the interdependencies of your people and the business systems on their working environment coupled with their welfare while they are working to achieve the business's strategy and vision. We all know that standard operating procedures and systems are critical to ensure we get quality outcomes and consistency in the delivery of our work. Equally if not more important is recognising the significance of cultivating a business culture centred on mutual respect. By fostering mutual respect, an environment of trust develops. Trust is one of the most important aspects of a working environment.

The value of employees

Like standard operating procedures, we all understand the importance of systems and why systems will give us that consistency in productivity and quality that our clients expect and deserve. But if you don't have employees who can use those systems effectively and to the best of their ability, you won't get that consistency in quality and service. Not getting the consistency causes conflict, and conflict inevitably contributes to increased anxiety, leading to an increased disassociation from the people and process, and in turn fosters a culture where other team members disassociate from that employee. It is the snowball theory: when you leave the psychosocial hazards unaddressed, no matter how small you believe them to be, they will grow and gather speed. This is not a trajectory you would like to find yourself managing, as it will eventually result in the good people who recognise their own value leaving and you being left to try to lead a team that is less than happy and not high performing.

As you can see, I am all about challenging the usual way, and I propose to do that again. Consider this: you decide to invest in a new piece of equipment for your business that we will call Zenn. Zenn has a price tag of $180,000. The sales brochure specifies that the use of Zenn be limited to 38 hours per week, and has a whole of life of 46 weeks. After 46 weeks Zenn has reached its lifespan and you are required to purchase another Zenn to replace the old one. The new Zenn will run in parallel with the old Zenn for two weeks prior to shutting the old one down.

Think about this. How realistic does this scenario sound? What consideration would you give to the purchase of Zenn – the careful research, selection, purchase and subsequent treatment? How much effort would you put into ensuring the storage and environment were correct, that Zenn was not subject to anything that could possibly disturb you getting the best return on investment. Okay, check your thoughts; are they something like, *I had best ensure that if I was going to invest in Zenn then ....* And you ensured there were lots of conditions on the purchase and how that machine is looked after once it is installed in your workplace, and the team training so that it has a positive return on investment, and the location within the business to ensure it is suitable, and so on.

Now shift the focus of your thinking; consider that you need to recruit a new team member. You review the position description and calculate the salary to be $100,000. For budgeting purposes you know you need to consider oncosts of employing and retaining that new team member – whether they work in the office or other areas, the oncost is similar. My question to you is: would you undertake the same amount of research and consideration for the recruitment and retention of a team member with a salary of $100,000 as you would do when purchasing Zenn. Depending on your business cost variables, your total cost of employing that team member probably equates to around $180,000 per annum. Would you be willing to invest as much or even more in recruiting and retaining a new team member as you would in purchasing Zenn? Your team members, after all, draw an annual salary, work 38 hours per week, and are available for productivity for approximately 46 weeks per year, accounting for public holidays, annual leave and other absences. Shifting your perspective in this pragmatic manner highlights the value of investing in your people, ensuring a safe and content workplace for their productivity, and that they are happy to be productive in a job they enjoy for an extended period. There will be times that employees leave and that is okay. What is important is to understand the departure.

Understanding employee departures

I challenge you to do some cost analysis on what I'd call 'voluntary employee departure'. The regrettable departures. These are the employees who don't feel heard or appreciated; they are the ones who want to feel empowered to get on with doing their job in the best possible way. Count the voluntary departures in the resignation area of your employee management system, and question the key driver of this behaviour. Why are they leaving, and what is driving them to go looking for another job? Let me assure you, money will be low on the list unless the team member had just graduated from an apprenticeship or traineeship, or is in a position that pays the minimum wage.

Look at the departure from the perspective that not only have you lost a valuable employee you will have also created a productivity void and financial cost that sits beside your opportunity cost. Really look closely from a holistic business ecosystem perspective. When you start to analyse the voluntary turnover, it's about what it costs you not only for that person to leave and to recruit and train the next person, but it is also the loss of company knowledge, and team cohesiveness. Put that systems thinking lens into your glasses when you do your reality check; what is lost in the energy that the employee brought to the group, the tacit knowledge and the opportunity cost of training the new person post recruitment?

We see daily that the behaviour of your team does not go unnoticed, particularly in the media. And we are aware that the media will look for and find a story when things go wrong. What you really would like is for them to report when things go *right*, to show how you are building a psychosocially safe culture. This will give you positive publicity – the long-term process of getting recognition when your value movement has become people-driven not financially driven. Be assured when your culture is people-driven it will also be positive for your finances.

Employees who like to work with their leaders, those who have effective leadership engagement, will have greater motivation to work happily in producing quality work more effectively and efficiently. Inherently effective leaders do not become effective overnight. Many leaders are initially employed for the technical skills they offer, and then adapt those technical skills as they progress into more senior roles. The people skills, formerly called soft skills, however, are the skills they had to try to learn through the process of observation, by being mentored, by attending professional development seminars and courses that gave them theory, and then applying what they had learned in practice to the best of their ability. When individuals work alongside a skilled leader, they often learn vicariously through mentorship – observing, reflecting and applying these teachings in a supportive setting. Here, the focus isn't on making mistakes, but on fostering a safe learning environment where errors are part of the growth process. This is an ideal approach that is valuable for any business, fostered through a no-blame culture, where people feel safe to speak up about mistakes rather than cover them up.

Employees who like to work with their leaders, those who have effective leadership engagement, will have greater motivation to work happily in producing quality work more effectively and efficiently.

It is also about doing away with the concept of busyness. I have rarely met a colleague or employee who, when asked if they are busy, respond with a no. There is a need for team members to have time to think, to be creative, to be adaptable, and to understand how they can contribute to making their jobs more purposeful, meaningful, and self-directed because they like to come to work. They like the company to be a success, but they don't like being told. Lack of inclusiveness and consultation is the primary driver of why there is a concept that people do not like change. Being told is a rejection of change; inclusiveness on the journey will allow the employees to think about the changes, understand their role and contribution, and adopt the change because they are part of it. Think about technology. The extent to which every person has adapted to and integrated technology into their daily routine since the turn of this century is phenomenal. Why have they adapted and adopted? Because they were involved in the decision making, taken on the journey, and explained the benefits. The same comes from employees, and therefore I encourage you, if you have a team member leave because 'they didn't like the changes', ask the question: how involved were they in the journey of the change consultation and implementation process? When brought on the journey, it is not about the employees all liking the changes. Many may not; however, by involving them in the process and having them understand through the consultation journey the purpose for the change and the positive impact it will have on their work environment, the implementation will be successful. Why? Because not only do they understand the reason for the change, they progressively come to own it. Having an employee depart due to a change factor may be more about your change process than the employee not liking change. It is worth considering.

It is rarely a single aspect of a leader that makes them effective or ineffective as an individual. It's a collection of behaviours and actions that the leader displays over a period that the employees either like or they don't like, can work with or not. It is the leader's ability to adapt, and understand the differences in their team members, what they need and how that can be met in a meaningful and impactful way, that makes a difference to creating a positive culture for happy employees.

Awareness of psychosocial hazards has become an immediate and explicit need of many businesses, particularly as companies are now being exposed and vilified in the media for some of the behaviours that now ex team members have been applying and which have been demonstrated to be inappropriate and causing hazards in the work environment. The failures of the past have now become more than risk management; it is also reputation management. Manage the risk, manage your company's reputation, and happy employees will protect your reputation.

Happy employees tend to be more hopeful and optimistic, and they are a critical part of your stakeholder ecosystem that ensures the success not only of your reputation but all of your business strategy.

Understanding job demands

Knowing your employees' job preferences is a significant contributing factor in creating a safe psychosocial workplace with a positive culture and happy employees. High or low job demands is one of the aspects that could potentially be a hazard. If you have a job that is repetitive and could be considered monotonous, allocating this role to a person who likes routine and prefers to do the same thing to perfection repeatedly may be ideal. However, to give the position to a person who thrives on diversity could be considered by them a mental hazard as they are not being stimulated to the extent that they enjoy their job.

I have observed and talked with the drivers of the big dump trucks on mine sites, hauling material every day. To me it is a repetitive and mundane job. However, when I speak with the drivers, they love it. The power of the truck engines, the weight of the load, the feeling of being in control of something that is so huge. That is what feeds their sense of achievement. When we discuss my work – keynote speaking, conducting workshops, writing books, facilitating strategic planning and coaching people to improve their leadership – I receive comments that usually start with *don't ask me to* ... 'Don't ask me to do any public speaking.' 'Don't ask me to try to plan anything to do with writing.' And the discussion goes on. It is about identifying and capitalising on strengths and, as I alluded to earlier, understanding the value each person has to contribute.

Although many repetitive types of jobs are being automated – automatic number plate recognition has overtaken data entry for speed cameras, parking fines and similar jobs; the Amazon warehouse for packing; autonomous freight trains – there are still significant roles that can be classified as monotonous. Autonomous rail and hauling vehicles work through the integration of robotic components, advanced software, GPS and internet connectivity, however an employee has to sit and watch a screen all day to ensure that there is not a glitch in the system that loses connectivity or that derails a vehicle for some other reason. Monitoring the screens for a 12-hour shift day in and day out could be considered by the diversity person, such as me, a low adaptability demand job and therefore it becomes a hazard. Conversely, think of Heidi who I spoke of earlier: she is a person who likes routine, who sees this as knowing what she needs to do and it not being physically or mentally demanding – she may like to work monitoring the screens and be quite happy. I will admit I do know it is more than watching the screens, it is knowing what to do when an incident occurs, however that is not the daily routine. Leading to create a happy workplace is about using the strengths of your employees. There is a company on the Sunshine Coast called iMend Tech where the leaders recognise the jobs are routine and tend to be repetitive: replacing broken phone screens and similar non-complex but very essential technology services. The leaders focus on trying to recruit people who like to have routine, and have discovered that employees who have intellectual and developmental challenges are their most highly sought after and valued. It is a symbiotic relationship where the work is predominately low demand and where the employees are happy because they have positive and meaningful employment; they enjoy the level of empowerment they have and the satisfaction of a phone that looks like new again, and know they will have a happy customer.

Similarly, job demands can be physical. I recall watching a large complex of holiday units being built in Darwin. As the most northern major city in Australia, Darwin has two seasons: the wet and the dry. During the build up to the wet the temperature is intense; it is regularly 34 degrees with 99% humidity and no relief from rain. The labourers who were installing metal Colorbond on the roofs of the units were under tight schedules because of the pending wet season and they were pressured to get the units watertight. I would watch them go for lunch; they would take their shirts off, wring out the sweat and put them back on hoping to be cool, then go to the sandwich shop for lunch. They would open the drink refrigerator, take out three or four bottles of electrolyte-laced drinks and drink a litre of the cooling liquid before even thinking about ordering food. That work environment is a situation where it could be deemed the labourers were under unreasonable physical and psychological pressure. The demands of the job were excessive because it was not one day that they did this highly demanding task, it was successive days spanning weeks. When I spoke to them they responded, 'We have to do it because if we don't get it done, done properly and done on time, we won't get paid properly or be hired for another job.'

> " Job demand is about balancing the intensity of demand on your employees' emotional, mental and physical capabilities and including them in these conversations.

Job demand is about balancing the intensity of demand on your employees' emotional, mental and physical capabilities and including them in these conversations. It may be that they enjoy the challenge, but it is equally important to recognise if the enjoyment is for a short period and the work is not enjoyable over a long period. Regular check-in discussions will help in understanding if the status has changed.

Understanding empowerment

As I commented above, empowerment is one of those words that has been around management dialogue and leadership circles for a long time but seldom is there an understanding of what it actually is. The short answer: it is about the amount of control and decision making an employee has over their specific job and their daily tasks. Observation of workflow and listening to dialogue are great indictors of empowerment. Some of the statements you may hear in the lunchroom will tell you the extent to which employees are being empowered. When you hear statements like, 'I wish I could just get on with what I have to do, instead of having to go back and check with him at each stage,' or maybe, 'If I get told one more time what to do, how to do it and why it needs to be done that way I am going to scream.' These statements indicate a low degree of empowerment, and as you can see they are not the most effective use of your employees' competencies and they are psychosocial hazard alert statements.

To be the best employees, your people want and need to have a say in how they do their work and have some control over when specific aspects are done. This is not giving them permission to miss deadlines; it is not indicating they do not need to meet targets. It is creating a work environment where they feel they can do the aspects that they have the energy for at the time. We all have aspects of our jobs that are boring and that we don't particularly like to do. However, being in control of what can be done and when within a broad framework increases the level of energy and motivation an employee has for their job and the potential for increased outcomes. This, in turn, has a direct relationship with their level of optimism and workplace happiness.

I was working with an executive team in the aviation industry to further build their leadership competencies. The Head of Commercial and Finance was a good example of not empowering her team. When I first started to work with her, I asked her about her team. She would tell me that she empowered them and that they had meaningful jobs. I could see that they were not happy, and the lunchroom discussion confirmed this. When I asked what the real challenge was, I was shocked by the answers, so much so that I asked a team member to repeat the response so I could write it down. She said, 'The problem with Marion is that nothing is ever good enough, we can do our best work or half a job and she will still find problems. What we do now is do the minimum and let her find a fault, and then we fix it up. It has made the process more time constrained, and the work is now boring as we are no longer allowed to think.' In this case, the leader's need for perfectionism (her words) has disempowered her people and led them to not only feel like robots but also seeking alternate employment. Yes, I recognised we had some work to do here, and it was a fun balance in the employees trusting that Marion would and could change her leadership style and them being prepared to stay to work with it. We were optimistic, and that served us well in the process.

Fostering optimism

As a result of a positive and safe work environment, your employees are likely to be optimistic, which allows them to build stronger adaptive and coping skills. In turn this means they are less likely to avoid decision making when they are faced with complex challenges or problems. This is because optimism involves reasoning, emotive and motivational components, which helps them build stronger reliance on and therefore relationships with colleagues. Building resilience and collaboration through optimism will happen when your employees know they have the support to not only work through their challenge but also if the decision is wrong, they can learn from it rather than feel anxiety and fear. This helps to build resilience in the employees and improved systems and processes as the mistakes are being addressed not covered up.

The level of your leaders' and employees' capacity to adapt to adverse events and cultivate resilience directly relates to the extent that they are able to bounce back from challenges and enhance the social dynamics in the workplace. The employees with increased resilience coupled with a reasonable dose of emotional intelligence will most likely be willing to help others build and maintain their positivity.

> A positive psychosocial safety culture is not something you get or buy; it is something you work on to build and maintain within a continuous improvement focus.

A positive psychosocial safety culture is not something you get or buy; it is something you work on to build and maintain within a continuous improvement focus. Culture can be positive, negative or neutral. Its foundation is in what your employees believe about its importance.

The challenge with identifying and managing psychosocial safety in your workplace is that different people inherently like to do different things and have different internal drivers. This is why it is important to know your people and to regularly put some science behind the way your leaders are building a positive workplace culture, one that is aligned with your business purpose and values.

Conclusion

It is important you recognise that even though your employees can't be perfect all the time, understanding where people are coming from, their point of view, what their needs are and how to meet them is understanding that employment is a two-way process. It's a give and take. It is understanding that the hazards are hazards if they are present repeatedly, in a way that will cause harm – it is your role to address this. Therefore, it is about the depth of your understanding of your employees' needs, as well as ensuring your employees understand your needs and those of the business. When these are aligned, the growth you're anticipating in your business will be achieved. When they are not aligned, you will spend a lot of time investing in recruitment and replacement. Additionally, there is possibly the cost of lawyers and Fair Work Commission issues as well as all the things that are reactionary and don't grow and develop your employees. It is really a proactive or reactive choice – and I can show you how to be proactive, which provides a better return for your business.

When you have happy employees you also have a profitable business through increased productivity. Happy people are productive people, and when people know what's required of them and have the skill to do it they will set about doing it in a way that makes them happy and gives you the return you are looking for. And they enjoy doing it. People who are allowed to get on and do their job in a psychosocially safe culture are a long way on the journey to being a happy employee and you are on the same path to getting the returns you are seeking.

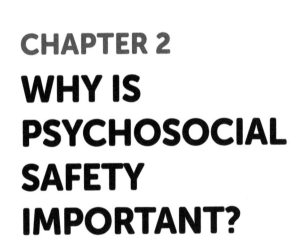

CHAPTER 2

WHY IS PSYCHOSOCIAL SAFETY IMPORTANT?

An environment where everybody can speak out

Food for thought: is it better to invest in hazard mitigation than to spend valuable finances on legal defence, and possibly compensation, and *then* hazard removal?

When your employees know that they will not be humiliated or otherwise punished for proposing or questioning ideas in a genuine way, when they know they can celebrate mistakes by learning from them and when they feel they will not be harassed, you as a leader know you are on the path to creating a psychosocially safe place fostering happy employees.

In research findings published in the *Harvard Business Review* on 22 November 2023 titled 'Research: When – and Why – Employee Curiosity Annoys Managers', the authors found that it is not as easy as fostering curiosity alone. They write that:

> they conducted a series of studies to understand when curiosity may lead to different reactions in the workplace. They found that curious employees were often seen by their leaders as insubordinate and, in turn, less likeable. However, curious employees who were politically skilled were not seen this way, where research has shown that curiosity can facilitate psychological safety, problem solving and innovation. They distinguished between constructive curiosity, which involved seeking information, knowledge, or learning by asking many provocative questions that don't have easy answers, and unconstructive curiosity, which involved seeking information, knowledge, or learning by asking too many questions and questions with easy answers. Their findings have implications for managers, who should ensure they're not dismissing employees expressing constructive curiosity, and employees, who should ensure they're not engaging in unconstructive curiosity.

This research illustrates that cultivating a workplace where everybody at all levels and in all roles can shine and speak out without fear creates a fruitful and productive business, but it is not as simple as telling them to ask questions. It is how the questions are structured and the purpose behind them, seeking answers to complex questions, and the approach to adopting curiosity. This is to say it is problem solving rather than being told what to do, which links in with seeking innovation and empowerment not micromanagement. These approaches are the micro-details in building a psychologically safe culture.

> Why is psychosocial safety important? Because it provides a better way of living and working.

Why is psychosocial safety important? Because it provides a better way of living and working. As I alluded to, I conducted multiple interviews when I was writing this book so I could provide multiple insights, not just those that I have gained over the past 20 years. The owners of mid-sized businesses and key leaders in large businesses and government that I spoke with all agreed on one thing. As employers, we can no longer expect our employees to come to work and leave all of their other worries of home and family at the 'office' entrance door. The work environment and expectations are changing, and it is now recognised that employing is about the whole person, understanding that out-of-work pressures and challenges do impact on the work and there is a need for a holistic view, for fostering flexibility, adaptability and collaborative discussions to ensure the best outcomes for everybody.

Good psychosocial safety is a powerful strategic position for your business when you set the environment up for your employees to be adaptive and feel empowered to collaborate in building a work environment they enjoy. This directly and positively impacts on performance and productivity. Having a focused psychosocially safe framework integrated into your business practices means you and your people can and will have the hard and uncomfortable conversations and they will not feel hard and uncomfortable. When done well, these conversations can be transformative for your employees, your working relationships and your whole business ecosystem. Psychosocial safety is one aspect of a holistic approach to business fitness.

An accountant friend puts it clearly and correctly when he tells me:

> there are four versions of fitness in our world; emotional, mental, physical and financial, and if we're looking after all of the pieces that we can in the emotional and the mental fitness sides of life, and we have a culture and environment that enables our staff to flourish, then I think we're giving them the best chance for success.

And they are giving *you* the best chance of success, for without your people your success factor significantly diminishes. Remember the challenge of trying to operate without them for 30 days. The aspect that can be added here as an overarching element is quality. We all know from a product perspective that quality gives a better return, and the same can be said for the work environment. A positive work environment contributes significantly to a work ecosystem that will enable your employees to develop high-calibre relationships and produce higher quality work and outcomes.

Allowing for the need to be compliant with any relevant psychosocial Code of Practice, the inherent value and importance of psychological safety cannot be underestimated in terms of employee wellbeing, which in turn contributes to increased collaboration as employees like to work together, they like the work and they like to celebrate the positive aspects of their achievements. Your employees will also want to learn from their mistakes; what went wrong, why it happened and what can be done to prevent it from happening again – a much sounder approach to continuous improvement than fearing they will be reprimanded or punished and therefore covering up the mistake. Failure to have an environment that acknowledges mistakes for what they are deprives your business of the opportunity to innovate, learn and enhance systems. It also denies employees the chance for psychological wellbeing. Unless the team member who made the mistake is self-serving and has narcissistic traits, they are likely to feel guilty about the mistake they made, and their level of anxiousness will increase if they do not feel they can safely speak up without adverse repercussions. Mistakes are just that; no one purposefully sets out to make a mistake, and if you enable employees to recognise, own and discuss the error, the likelihood of the mistake occurring again is minimal if not completely mitigated. Your focus should be on achieving outcomes rather than looking for fault and blame; this is where you will gain the best from your people and your business investment.

Self-awareness in leaders

What you are really looking for in a psychosocially safe environment are high levels of employee engagement through building self-awareness, trust, empowerment and adaptability. Building an environment where there is comfort in innovation, employees at all levels learning about themselves and from their personal mistakes; being accountable for self-management and understanding what that means for every one of the employees in the business.

Self-awareness, respect and trust are vital aspects of your safety and business culture. High levels of self-awareness are important for leaders as it helps them to understand themselves and other employees better and enables them to make more efficient decisions because they know their strengths and where they need support. This means the leaders make better choices by being aware of their own personality strengths, their habits and their weaknesses, and how these impact their colleagues and team members.

In being able to manage their own emotions and behaviour, and to inspire and motivate others with their optimism and confidence, the leaders' high level of self-awareness will assist in increasing awareness of the extent of psychosocial safety and psychosocial hazards in the workplace. Self-awareness also allows them to recognise the needs, preferences and expectations of different employees and to adjust the way they engage with people. This helps to establish the foundations of a safe, open environment for business growth. High levels of self-awareness also allow leaders to be open to feedback with a willingness to learn from their mistakes and successes, as well as to seek constructive criticism and advice from others. It is not about knowing it all as a leader, it is about knowing what questions to ask and who to ask to ensure the correct answers are found and implemented.

Self-awareness also raises emotional intelligence. Emotional intelligence is the ability of your leaders to identify and manage their own emotions and recognise those of others. Leaders with a high level of emotional intelligence are essential for psychosocial safety, as it enables them to build trust, empathy and rapport with their team and to handle complex and challenging situations with calmness and resilience.

> The seven years of research I did into effective leadership showed self-awareness is one of the most valuable qualities for leaders as it helps them to lead themselves and others more effectively.

The seven years of research I did into effective leadership showed self-awareness is one of the most valuable qualities for leaders as it helps them to lead themselves and others more effectively. Self-awareness is not a fixed attribute that leaders either have or don't have; they can work on developing awareness and improve with focused application, as well as reflection and seeking feedback from others such as peers, managers, team members and mentors. The scientific approach to this is starting with a SHEPS assessment. This will measure, among other attributes, the level of self-awareness. And by being aware, leaders can leverage their strengths and optimise the strength of their team to have a positive, happy and productive work environment. This balance is critical to ensuring that the work environment is safe, and is the foundation to establishing and maintaining strong, trusting and respectful relationships.

Trust is vital

Trust is a vital element in the webs of connection that build your safe workplace. It is a strange thing, trust – some people will say it should be given, and the team members work with that foundation until it is broken - which we hope is never; and there are others that say that the team members must prove that they are worthy of trust before it is given. Which camp are you sitting in? Be honest with yourself. When you have the answer, consider why it needs to be like this and why it works. True, sound, trustful relationships ensure an equitable balance of fun and seriousness, innovation and focus is maintained. It is one of the many intangible aspects of a happy workplace that can't be described when it is there but can be described when it is not there. Trust is an attribute that is felt more than observed. It is often attributed to the behaviour of individuals, and accepted when given without a second thought. However, when a transgression is strong enough, the lack of trust spreads like spilled coffee across all employees and soaks in, staining the level of safety they thought they had. This is evident in one of the nation's most complex and controversial recent court proceedings; known across Australia as the 'Australian Parliament House sexual misconduct case'. There have been legal trials for allegations of sexual assault, which have been aborted. The reasons given, through multiple media channels, for the two criminal trials being aborted are mental health reasons and misconduct. There are also multiple defamation trials with conflicting evidence. As I write this, the proceedings have completed. However, what is evident is trust in knowing what truth actually is and managing the aftermath of where a psychosocial hazard has caused adverse outcomes to the parties involved is complex and challenging. Even the Judge, as reported in the *Sydney Morning Herald* on 21 December 2023, said as 'an insight into his approach to deciding the case, [Justice] Lee said that "one of the challenges in this case, it seems to me, is that the two principal witnesses [Lehrmann and Higgins] have real credit issues" and "various parts of each witness's evidence simply can't be accepted, it seems to me"'. There are no winners when risks become hazards and the hazards are not effectively managed or mitigated. There are destroyed people and reputations, and the ability for relationships to be regained to the level that they were prior to the incident is near impossible, both for the people directly involved as well as the colleagues, leaders, and associates in the work environment. This is a sad case of hazards not being managed, and the subsequent truth being told as the person sees it from their perspective. The trust has shattered the relationships and reverberated through the hallways so badly that the repercussions of voluntary and involuntary departures will ripple through Parliament House for a long time to come.

> When a *lack of trust* hazard is present, it has potential to adversely impact if not negate the collaborative culture that is being built and the positive psychosocial environment you're trying to achieve.

As this case illustrates, when broken, trust is very difficult, if not impossible, to regain to the levels required to build a psychosocially safe and empowered environment because there will be residue anchoring bias. Remember, I wrote about anchoring bias previously. This is where you have one aspect brought to your attention and seek other things to support it. In this case, where the trust has been broken, the likelihood of employees seeking reinforcement as to why it should not be rebuilt is heightened. This is saying, when the trust is shattered, employees will look actively to seek out other behaviours to support reasons not to work with specific team members and to not build trust again with the person or team that broke the trust. Lack of trust is not by itself a psychosocial hazard. It is the behaviours that the employees display around this that morphs into a psychosocial hazard for that employee or team. This is often seen around how work is organised: increased supervision coupled with low employee job control and sometimes too much or too little support, as described in the aviation case study above. When a *lack of trust* hazard is present, it has potential to adversely impact if not negate the collaborative culture that is being built and the positive psychosocial environment you're trying to achieve.

Building trust and collaboration

I am not saying you cannot have robust debate in case it breaks trust; nor am I saying that healthy conflict and collaboration are enemies. I am saying it is about awareness of the conflict, its root cause and the purpose it is serving. Conflict may be as simple as your employees having strong and varying opinions in relation to an innovation, process or change; and it is how this variance in opinion is managed and discussed that is important – not that there is conflict present but how it is managed. In fact, constructive conflict can be a healthy collaborative approach to problem solving. It is diversity in action. Understanding another person's perspective or position can be the platform for critical and analytical thinking and is the foundation of democratic decision making. When the risk matrix is being established and tested on large infrastructure and construction projects, I will often develop complex and contentious scenarios that have potential for opposing views and diversified opinions. The purpose is to workshop the scenarios to enable and facilitate robust and focused debate with diametrically opposed opinions. This is a healthy approach to understanding each of the stakeholders' thoughts and positions and to gain insights as to the risk likelihood, and consequences of that risk. Healthy debates also ensure a project management or mitigation strategy can be developed as the process is conducted knowing there is potential for things to go wrong.

Rather than fostering a culture of toxic positivity or the need to all agree, establishing a structured process with robust debate is much healthier for business growth and employee development. Toxic positivity is when we deny, minimise or invalidate the emotional experience of one of our employees, including difficult emotions that as leaders we feel we are not trained to manage, and try and put a positive perspective on all that is happening. These difficult emotions could be failed expectations, frustration expressed by the employee at not being able to achieve what they wanted to achieve or expressing grief due to the loss of a family member, pet or material possession that held a significant meaning.

We will all experience pain, failure, loss or disappointment at work, and not allowing this to be expressed is as destructive as any other psychosocial hazard. Some of the most difficult conversations are the ones that we can't necessarily be prepared for. The belief that only positive discussions can occur actually fosters a culture where psychosocial hazards arise, but are hidden with the potential to fester. This is because balanced contributions are hidden, due to the expectation that all should be positive. The feeling of pain and disappointment, the fear of making a mistake or not achieving a milestone is not expressed in meetings, and therefore the likelihood of genuine expression of emotion, challenge and even celebration will also be dampened. This approach can also compound into the person being subject to management of poor performance for not contributing at meetings, not because they did not want to, but because they did not feel safe to speak for fear of either saying the wrong thing, or what they do say being misinterpreted. Is this the type of restrained culture you are seeking to build? I think not.

Balance is important and it is gained and maintained when your company values and principles are set out clearly, and through recognising that it's not a set-and-forget strategy. The principles need to be continuously communicated, applied and subtly recognised. When this is done, your employees will learn how to apply them in a safe environment and integrate them into their daily work practices. This approach is important particularly when recruiting so new people don't come into a skewed culture. As part of the induction they need to be introduced to and understand the acceptable workplace interactions and behaviours and see them being modelled.

I interviewed a team member from a well-respected, award-winning legal firm. I asked her if her leaders promoted a positive workplace culture that encourages trust, respectful behaviours and quality communication. She told me that the directors are very focused on ensuring employees are trained not only in the skillset required but also the expected standards and culture. The business distinguishes itself by selling a 'premium' service, which means on an internal level employees are expected to apply high standards of respect with each other and then outwardly in the quality of work they do and in their interactions with their clients.

This is reflected in what she referred to as the 'values' posters displayed in the office to remind employees of the behaviours that are acceptable and those that are not. She explained that 'operating "above the line" in our practice means having ownership, accountability and responsibility in your role and participation in culture. Blame, excuses and denial in the workplace are not accepted as they are "below the line" behaviours.' A succinct way of remembering what is and is not acceptable behaviour.

Their ability to establish a no-blame culture and collaborate to embed practices to build a psychosocially safe workplace does not mean the employees are not accountable for their actions and behaviour. A positive no-blame culture *does not* remove accountability. Accountability is putting your hand up and saying I made the mistake and let's find a way to mitigate what caused it so it doesn't happen again. It is about analysing mistakes through a root cause approach, using systems thinking, concentrating on the problem rather than focusing on the person – the employee who made the mistake already feels bad enough for what happened. And really all the employee wants is to understand what went wrong and why, and contribute to developing and implementing a system, approach or process to ensure that the mistake is understood and not repeated. This is one approach of combining your no-blame culture with accountability. It is a process of learning and implementing a combination of risk mitigation and business improvement practices. This valuable approach to analysis and fostering innovation involves cultivating a 'no-blame' culture, which often serves as a catalyst for improvement. While mistakes shouldn't be the sole driving force, learning from them followed by implementing strategies for enhancement minimises employee stress and anxiety in a continuous-improvement setting and increases their commitment to quality. This approach also cultivates stronger, more resilient employees. Adopting such an approach creates a collaborative team deeply invested in the journey, fostering robust conversations within a safe, supportive environment. It enables the pursuit and implementation of improvements driven by the right reasons.

Using this approach is one aspect of building a psychosocial hazard–free environment to motivate employees to want to contribute more, resulting in a high-performance team. The employees feel safe to step up with a different or disruptive idea, knowing they will not be bullied or ridiculed. They can only do this, however, when they know that the culture, and specifically their leader, supports this approach. I checked this safety concept when I was having a chat with a leader of a moderate-sized IT company that has employees in multiple states. She told me that they:

> all work together as much as we work for one another. Steve might be the boss of the company but we are all on the same level and we all look after each other. They help me and I work with them, and we ensure that decisions are based on the priorities of the team and client and what is needed as a priority and who needs it.

In this company's culture they work hard to maintain there is no room for 'I'. It is how they best support each other no matter what the need. This ensures that no one is alone with a challenge, and they all feel supported. I suggested to her that this type of collaborative and empowered culture would take a fair bit to manage. She told me they consciously work on it each day. Is this a collaborative culture or a supportive culture? I suggest it is both, and it is a culture they are developing to ensure hazards are identified and managed before they have potential to become risks.

Collaboration and hybrid work

The concept that collaboration means all stakeholders need to be consulted and everybody in the consultation circle needs to agree is a *falsehood*. Collaboration is about the way your team works to develop better relationships and builds effective inter- and cross-communication to effectively share information and solve challenges. This approach has become more evident with the hybrid work environment. I was doing research about the impact of the decreased presence of employees in the office as a result of the restrictions imposed through managing the pandemic. A social worker I spoke with said it enabled her to balance her priorities; she could manage her caseload more effectively as working from home allowed focused, uninterrupted time to update case notes and have confidential client phone calls without managing the busyness of the people in the office. She explained further that they physically had a smaller working space now due to the assumption that not all employees would be in the office at any one time, and it was a struggle when they were. It became a situation where they would roster to work from home so they could feel more in control of managing the workloads and the office desk space. In-person collaboration was on an as-needs basis depending on the resources available and the client need.

Conversely, when speaking with a Project Director who was overseeing the design of a new billion-dollar project concurrently with early environmental investigation and community stakeholder identification, the multiple moving parts of the project were potentially suffering as was the speed to market. This was because there had been a shift from collaborative and vicarious learning by hearing what is happening with other parts of the project while working in the office to being transactional because there was isolation thinking and collaboration as was thought 'necessary'. The spontaneous conversations sparking incremental improvements and areas to be alert to were missing.

He said:

the impact of hybrid working is slowing the project down as things tend to be done in isolation, and the ability to get a high degree of interaction and collective innovation is much lower. This is because there have to be scheduled meetings that take longer, and there are not established relationships, so the elements of getting people to talk and share ideas is difficult.

The outcome of this absence of engagement is a lack of meaningful relationships being formed, a low degree of innovative thinking and new team members leave as they have not developed the required skills through on the job mentoring and are choosing not to integrate. There is nothing here that shouts *we all have to agree*; what is essential in collaboration is to agree on the purpose of a conversation, the objectives and the agenda. Unfortunately, this is potentially not occurring in this situation with the demise of collaboration and the ever-present transactional interactions.

To always have consensus would not only stifle any creative or innovative discussion, it could push your team into groupthink, which the transactional approach has a tendency to foster. You have probably heard of groupthink; it is a concept developed in 1972 by a psychologist named Irving Janis when he saw teams having robust discussions but developing a decision bias based on the desire of the group members' need to have harmony, member acceptance and therefore conformity. He realised they were not giving the best input to their discussions, nor were they arriving at the best outcomes. They were simply feeling obligated to take the path of least resistance so they could remain members of the group. This is not a healthy dynamic in a business that needs to be innovative to stay ahead of trends and grow and develop while putting employee welfare as their number one priority. It also has the potential to develop a psychosocial hazard through lack of inclusion.

Managing risks and obligations

I take this opportunity to remind you this is not a legal book and does not provide legal advice, however with all the legislative acts and associated regulations and codes of practice there are compliance obligations. To sound very formal, I will say that addressing psychosocial safety is a way of illustrating your positive duty of care to manage and mitigate the risks that your employees are or could be exposed to that may cause them anxiety and stress. To explain the same statement differently: the employer has the responsibility to identify psychosocial hazards and risks and, as far as reasonably practical, implement controls and manage risks to prevent the hazards from occurring. Pretty heavy stuff, isn't it?

We all know each person is different and recognise that the ability of our employees to tolerate and manage stress varies, so you may feel managing psychosocial hazards and risks is rather complicated. Let me assure you that you are not alone in feeling this. Firstly, let me share a conversation I was included in at a Chamber of Commerce function, and then provide insight from a very senior team member of a state government-owned statutory corporation. The essence of both of the conversations was around flexible work arrangements and particularly the value or otherwise of the open plan office and the continued value of such when coupled with flexible work arrangements. The open plan was initially designed so people could connect with each other and had been in place for some time. It was retained so that employees did not feel they were isolated or working alone given the hybrid arrangements, the acceptance of a low number of people in the office on a daily basis and the increased number of people working at home. Some liked it. Others said they are so used to working without people in close proximity now that working back in an open plan would stress them out and they prefer to work from home all the time.

According to the *Fair Work Act 2009*, the acceptance or denial of an employee's desire to work from home must pass the reasonableness test. These types of tests are usually dependent on lots of factors, including contracts and agreements of employment and the circumstances of the individual. This illustrates the complexity of managing the social factors and mental wellbeing of working from home, which is a social isolation factor, balanced with the loss of vicarious coffee machine discussions, which are a social connectivity aspect of working in an office. It also illustrates the multiple gaps in trying to build positive workplace relationships which occur when people are present, the potential to unknowingly foster high stress loads, and interpersonal conflict because of the formerly acceptable open plan discussions that are now no longer acceptable to some.

Stress is something more personal that relates to feeling tension and worry. It is often where we feel uncomfortable about something such as our personal relationships because we work away for extended periods of time, sometimes our finances, or work-related stress from hours worked in high pressure, a high degree of negativity, or as I said earlier, workplace fear and lack of trust.

Stress is a little like pollution on buildings. Let me explain my theory of Pollution Stress. Visualise your daily walk to the coffee shop, and you walk past a beautiful sandstone heritage building.

You notice that something is happening as there is scaffolding around the building, and then early the following week you see the building has been pressure cleaned and all of the pollution is gone. The building almost radiates with the browns, reds and crème of the beautiful clean sandstone. You didn't notice the pollution building up because the car emissions and other atmospheric pollution were quietly settling on it daily. Well, sometimes stress follows the same pattern in your and your employees' bodies – there are incremental changes and pressures in your employees' work and family life. The layers of stress will build up, polluting their ability to stay calm and focused. If you are not aware of the buildup, one day you will notice that their behaviours are different and there will need to be drastic and signification action to counter the stress levels. Unfortunately, should this occur with your employees it is not as simple as constructing some scaffolding and having a pressure clean, however it is important to have the support structures around so employees know they can manage issues and gain assistance to avoid getting to those levels. What I am suggesting is you raise your conscious awareness of the repeated levels of stress that are slowly eroding your and your employees' resilience and building up to become a central stressor. What has happened above with the open plan office is the potential hazard of loneliness. This has to be counterbalanced as the change in expectation and workplace dynamics has contributed to a new stress factor of noise overload.

> A strong psychologically safe culture requires a focused effort to establish and maintain, however once in place is a powerful strategic positioning of your company.

A strong psychologically safe culture requires a focused effort to establish and maintain, however once in place is a powerful strategic positioning of your company. When in place, a strong psychologically safe culture also builds a sense of ownership and wellbeing for your employees as they know they can be adaptive and feel empowered to collaborate. Building a work environment they enjoy directly and positively impacts on their performance and productivity and the financial bottom line for your business.

Staying connected

According to the Fair Work Ombudsman, workers who have been with their employer for more than 12 months have the right to request flexible work arrangements, and as an employer you are required to consider their request. Can you refuse? Yes, you can – on 'reasonable business grounds'. Like all legal jargon, 'reasonable business grounds' can be interpreted multiple ways, but Fair Work indicates that if it relates directly to the person and this aligns with cost, efficiency, productivity or customer service, you *may* (it doesn't say will) have grounds to refuse. I challenge you, however: do you want your employees applying to the Fair Work Commission for assistance in resolving a dispute if you have rejected their request? I suggest this is not a good move for your business reputation, employee morale or the associated time, economic loss and opportunity costs.

So what does a flexible hybrid work environment look like? It is what you make it – it depends on how you achieve your business goals within the negotiated employment conditions. I know this sounds a little difficult and not very specific, however it is a baseline to start from, to start to understand your employee business strategy and the impact this request will have on it, your leadership culture and the sentiment of your employees; it shows if your compass is pointing in the right direction to have happy employees.

Hard and uncomfortable conversations

Having a focused framework and integrating these identified behaviours into your business-as-usual practices means you and your employees can and will have the hard and uncomfortable conversations. But they don't have to be hard or difficult.

What is interesting about these conversations is the difference between those leaders who have actively worked to manage and include the Code of Practice as a positive approach and those who have seen it as compliance. Interestingly, there appears to be a generational gap, particularly with those who could be classified as Generation Z, in relation to behavioural and workplace expectations. This is evident both in the public sector and the private sector, however the approaches are different.

The public sector leaders that I spoke with post the acceptance of flexible and hybrid workplaces, experienced a loss of new graduates due to limited opportunities for them to develop and interact with senior personnel. Consequently, the new graduates relied heavily on courses for information, and the leaders who were mentors were either not in the office or did not appear to be available for mentoring when they were. This led to a reduced ability by the graduates to apply their knowledge effectively, have someone willing to listen to ideas and learn from mistakes with a structured proactive approach. This challenge persisted because there were few, if any, senior employees available for timely consultation, due in part to working from home, and also to the increased need for meetings as mentioned previously.

In the private sector, Roz White sees the generational impact also and recognises that the newer Z generation has a completely different thought process. Roz says:

> We've always heard that all these young ones think they know better and they should just, you know, do it our way. Well, I don't have that mindset. My thought is their new thoughts and the way they think, it might be alien to the way we think but we've got something to learn. I think they need to maybe give a little bit too and understand more about why we do things this way. But we need to understand we need to be adapting. It is a two-way process.
>
> If you're not relevant to this new generation, which is our future workforce, you'll never have loyal employees who will feel fulfilled, will feel valued, will feel respected. They feel respected when they're heard and they feel respected because they're acknowledged.
>
> Some of them have very enthusiastic and ambitious goals. Let's keep that enthusiasm, but say, 'Okay, I love your enthusiasm about that. But here are the reasons why you need to slow down and take these steps, because by taking the time and gaining your experience, you will be a better professional, in time.'

As you can see, when the integration is done well it can be transformative for your employees and your business as a whole. I ask you to think about your mindset; which approach do you have and is this the best for your business? It may not be either of the examples I have provided, and it is worth investing the reflection time to see what strategies you have that are retaining or losing your people. It is also a critical juncture as it will not be long before Generation Alpha will be entering the workforce and that will require more considerations that may not yet have been contemplated.

Indicators of when there is not a psychosocially safe environment

The behavioural indicators that are almost immediately evident when there is not a psychosocially safe environment are:

- increased absenteeism
- growing anxiety
- poor or absent decision making.

Let's look at these three aspects of psychological safety.

Increased absenteeism

Whichever source you choose to use in measuring absenteeism, it is always a cost. In financial terms it costs Australian businesses a significant amount. *CFO Magazine* posted online on 22 May 2023 an article by Nina Hendy referring to a survey by Frost and Sullivan, quoting the financial cost as an eyewatering '$24.2 billion in lost productivity the previous year', being 2022. This amount is four times higher than the figure Safe Work published in 2016, when it was $6.3 billion per annum. Even allowing for the compounding effect of inflation, the financial figures alone show that there is something amiss with the social and mental wellbeing of our employees. This is the financial cost; there is also a need to consider the compounding cost on family relationships, increased stress levels and decreasing resilience contributing to anxiety levels. The impact on the individual and others I would suggest is unquantifiable, however its constant presence is felt as strongly as high humidity; enveloping everybody. I was in a doctor's surgery some weeks ago and a lady who I guessed was in her late 30s to early 40s was asked about her medication. She responded by telling the triage nurse that although she was embarrassed to admit it, she was taking medication for anxiety and depression. The nurse responded: 'That's okay, everybody is these days – it's nothing to be embarrassed about.' I reflected on this short exchange of words and wondered if the nurse responded that way in an effort to make the patient feel less anxious, or was a very large percentage of the population really having to take medication for high levels of anxiety and depression? According to the Australian Bureau of Statistics, in the results of their National Study of Mental Health and Wellbeing for the two-year period to 2022, '42.9% of people aged 16–85 years had experienced a mental disorder at some time in their life'. This means that on average, half of your employees or every second person you walk past in the street is or has experienced a mental wellbeing challenge with the majority of those cases being anxiety.

What is contributing to this? Is it that our employees and the citizens of our communities have not been able to rebuild from the challenges experienced during the pandemic, and if this is the case, what are the barriers, and what should we be doing about it? Remember as leaders it comes under the duty of care banner in the accountability corner of our quadrant.

Growing anxiety

Anxiety has many contributing factors which are different for different people, however the presence or perceived presence of psychosocial hazards can contribute to the levels of concern and worry. Some of the influencing factors in your workplace include excessive workloads, poor organisational change management, aggression and harassment. These attributes contribute to your employees' feelings of being overwhelmed, stressed, exhausted – and can if left unaddressed lead to breakdowns and/or burnout. External life factors can also contribute to a compounding feeling of anxiety; for example, rising interest rates and the cost of living coupled with fears around job security can result in confusion and your employees trying to choose between competing priorities. Balancing personal wellbeing, including family time and exercise, alongside meeting job demands, which might necessitate working longer hours due to absenteeism among other employees, presents a complex situation. This confusion often makes leaders resort to stress-related responses in their leadership rather than thoughtful and focused responses. Recognising this dynamic is crucial, and taking steps to address it marks a positive move forward.

One of the very effective leaders I spoke with, and have mentioned previously, is Roz White, a company director employing 500. Or as Roz puts it, 'I have a family of 500'. Roz worked with the UniSC's Thompson Institute to develop and implement mental health and wellbeing training. According to their website:

> UniSC's Thompson Institute addresses society's most pressing mental health issues. We integrate world-class research, clinical services and education under one roof, because it enables fast translation of research breakthroughs into practice. Everything we do is underpinned by neuroscience. This uncovers promising new insights into mental health and how it is linked to our brain structure and function.

Having implemented the training across all the stores, Roz felt there was a need for another level of support for her key leadership team to bring back the energy they always had. It appeared they had lost the trademark customer-focused happy spring in their step that Whites IGA is renowned for. Developing and delivering a bespoke program specifically for the leadership team to focus on what was important to them at a personal level, Roz recognised that 'if we could find a way to sustain our leaders on a personal level, then they would become stronger and they would be better leaders by building the core strength of their personal and emotional resilience'. Working this into daily practices, building the resilience resulted in 'a higher level of consciousness and awareness about the importance of focusing on people'. The short-term impact on the business is evident, however the long-term impact and sustainability of the practices is still being built and assessed.

Poor or absent decision making

Poor or absent decision making is not only a thief of effectiveness and efficiency in building a high-performance team, it is a sure indicator of poor leadership.

Why do I say this? Think about it. What really happens when decisions are delayed or avoided? The first thing that some of the employees do is start to create a reason or self-serving truth around it. You would have heard some of these discussions – Oh! The reason that they are not making a decision is ... or the reason the decision is delayed it so they can [fill in the blank to suit your own perception]. Gossip and incorrect truths not only steal time, they create a level of negativity in the work environment that can, if left unchecked, contribute to increased anxiety. What else happens? Lots of things actually; not many of them positive. Often there are only three main reasons that critical decisions haven't been made or have been delayed. In most cases, it is because the leader does not have the capacity to make the decision, has been asked to make the decision without sufficient delegation, or is avoiding endorsing the decision because the decision to be made is the least favoured by the people who have to receive the news and/or implement the decision.

So what does this look like in practice? The decision is delayed, therefore employees become unclear as to what they should be doing pending the decision. They know they need to be working, however because there is a low degree of clarity on the focus areas, they might work on what they like to do, not what has to be done, as they are not sure what has to be done. There is a possibility they make an assumption on what decision is going to be made and will work on what they think should happen, which quite often results in the wrong work being done or duplication because someone else is working on the same aspect of the project but they don't know as there is no direction. What really happens is employees try to look productive while they are masking their anxiety and worry about job security. Some may even look for another job, depending on the magnitude of the decision and the timeline that the decision has been delayed.

Transparency is key here. Tell the team that the decision cannot be made and why, no excuses, because this increases the leader's credibility and the employees' respect for the leader. It shows the leader is human. Coupled with this, ensure that there is clarity given to the workers about what is expected from them while the decision is being delayed. Are they to continue on the work they are doing? Are they to assist other employees who are not waiting on the decision? Or, as was with one project I was associated with, do the employees take leave on the assumption that should approval be given, no leave can be taken in the coming 12 months due to the importance of the project?

The critical aspect is to recognise that no or delayed decisions create uncertainty and lost productivity, which increases anxiety, a significant psychosocial hazard in the workplace.

Conclusion

Based on what you have just read, I am sure you have been reassured that not only is psychosocial safety important, you are also aware of the impact on your business when it is left unaddressed. The financial, cultural and relationship impacts are immeasurable and felt as a ripple effect over a long period of time. The intangibles of trust, respect and integrity can be eroded, stress build-up compounded like pollution, and the impact of inappropriate behaviours creates a lasting ripple effect. These reasons, along with what you have read above, are the motivational foundations to find out where you really sit when it comes to having a psychosocially safe work environment. Not what you think is occurring, but the factual evidence. This can be achieved through a scientific approach of finding out through measurement.

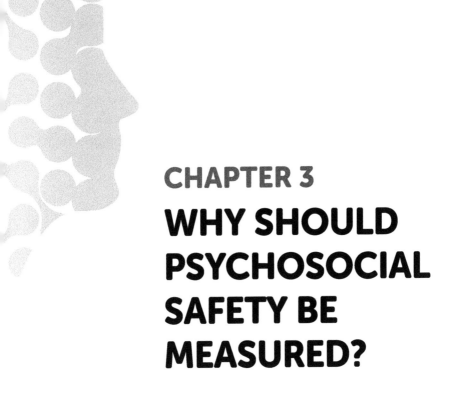

CHAPTER 3

WHY SHOULD PSYCHOSOCIAL SAFETY BE MEASURED?

The simple answer to this question is: because it is sound business practice. The long answer is provided below.

Identifying possible psychosocial hazards in the work environment

Toxic cultures and toxic positivity, where all is good on the surface because problems are not made explicit, are still ever-present in many workplaces. We would like to think that this is not the case, however the recurring reports in the media reinforce that believing we have all been working on building safe work environments that are psychosocially balanced is falsely optimistic.

The reason I am aware of this has been demonstrated earlier in this book through some of the stories I have shared. It was genuinely surprising to me that, on several occasions, the perspectives of the GM, CFO or business owner differed significantly from those of the employees. This indicated a clear disparity between what the employer believed was being implemented in their business and the reality of what was occurring in the work environment.

This wasn't always the situation, however what was interesting were the cases where there was misalignment, or possibly the existence of psychosocial hazards in the workplace:

- Firstly, the people being interviewed asked not to be identified if they were an employee, and if it was the GM or CEO they asked for the company not to be identified.

- Secondly, there was awareness that the business culture was not as good as it should be and they did not want this known to the greater public.

Thinking that there are possible psychosocial hazards in the work environment and not acting to find out if this is truth or gossip is like an ostrich putting its head in the sand because it has become all too hard. Avoidance is not only a potential violation of laws and codes of practice if the hazard does exist, it flags the start of the end for the business, and is also how employers can unwittingly end up responding to a Fair Work claim. I am aware that statement sounds harsh, however it is the truth that we need to face and act on, to prevent it eventuating.

> Thinking that there are possible psychosocial hazards in the work environment and not acting to find out if this is truth or gossip is like an ostrich putting its head in the sand because it has become all too hard.

Measuring and monitoring

As you have already read if you started at the beginning of the book, measuring psychosocial safety gives you data that identifies areas that need priority actions. Measuring and monitoring and conducting performance evaluation and analysis is the function of SHEPS, an approach that aligns with Section 9 of ISO 45003.[2] This is a relatively new standard that aims to provide frameworks and support of psychosocial health and safety in the workplace, through formal structures around managing mental health and social wellbeing. Being relatively new, many are not comfortable

---

2   ISO 45003 is the global standard guide for managing psychological and social health and wellbeing in the workplace, as part of an occupational health and safety management system. ISO (International Organization for Standardization) is a worldwide federation of national standards bodies.

in speaking up about it. Again this can be a combination of the culture in the workplace, generational expectations and employee expectations, among other drivers that are specific to the individual business.

The baby boomer generation have invested a significant amount of their life in a work environment where they were not supported or given the opportunity to speak about social and mental wellbeing. They lived by the mantra of *just get on with it*. This is illustrated in a chat I was having with an employee at one of the businesses where I was doing a culture health check. It was not a formal interview, more a chat over coffee and cake. I asked the lady – who I will refer to as Jennifer – how well she liked her job and if she would change anything, what would it be. Jennifer would be classified as a baby boomer, and I was astounded at her response:

> I love the work I do, but my two supervisors bully me a lot and expect me to do all the stuff they don't like to do. But I have been bullied all my life so I have come to expect it.

Well, my heart dropped into the red boots I was wearing that day, and I picked up my coffee cup to drink, buying time to think about the best way to respond to this. What surprised me was not only did Jennifer accept the bullying, she expected it to be an everyday part of her role. I was totally stunned; the business espoused an open-door policy, and Jennifer wouldn't report it because she saw it as an acceptable leadership practice.

This is a good example of not assuming employees know about and are comfortable with your open-door policy. They might know it is there, but they may not know what it really means or believe it is there for *them*. How do you know this? How do you find out?

Establishing a baseline similar to what SHEPS provides is both your culture health barometer and your compass point of where your focus needs to be as a priority in ensuring psychosocial safety.

> Depending on the business culture, sometimes SHEPS is the only way the information can be obtained.

ISO 45003 provides the risk-management guidelines that help you understand and implement effective controls to promote social and mental wellbeing in your business. The standard identifies the same base areas as the Code of Practice, such as areas of work-related stress that can lead to harm. SHEPS complements this by providing specific information that can identify if there are behaviours being applied in the workplace that are not openly evident, and the results allow the data to be a solid basis for consultation about what needs to be addressed and how the expectations can be met. Depending on the business culture, sometimes SHEPS is the only way the information can be obtained.

This was evident when I was recently working on an international project to build a high-performance team for a merged private and government-owned entity and I came across the following situation. A female engineer working in a male-dominated environment wrote a paper on how the department could become innovative and a leader in their field. She gave the paper to the head of her department, who took the paper but admonished her for working on something that was not her daily task. When she applied for a promotion, she was not successful and was not given feedback as to why. She then applied for a position in another department which was two levels higher than she was working at and was successful, however her current leader refused to release her to the new position.

Through our confidential processes we were able to identify this inappropriate behaviour. When the head of department was approached in relation to this process, he identified her as an employee who was not committed to her role as she spent too much time doing things that were supposed to be his job, such as process improvement and new opportunities, and therefore was not doing the job she was paid to do. The leader failed to recognise how the employee was value adding to the department, failed to ask when she found time to do the extra work which in fact she was doing at home at night, and then in effect punished her for her extra contributions. Without assessing the leadership and being able to gain confidential feedback, that company would have not only lost significant innovation that added value, it would not have recognised the extent that the departmental head was in need of leadership training, coupled with the high likelihood of the valued employee exiting the business. One of those voluntary departures that I was talking about earlier.

This is a pertinent example of the value of an independent person getting behind the façade of the culture in a non-threatening way. Fundamental to this process – and for you when measuring your business culture – is for your employees to understand why you are choosing to measure their safety and the importance of hazard identification. To ensure success, it is essential that the focus and message is a positive one. You will be addressing mental wellbeing and social factors at work, which is not something everyone is comfortable with.

The survey is about your leaders and employees, and allowing them to have their say; it is gathered confidentially, managed independently and the feedback provided sensitively. The results demonstrate in a valid way the vulnerable areas and the strengths of your leaders and their team, and identify some of the stumbling points that are not allowing some team members to perform at their best. When members not performing at their best occurs, the levels of stress and uncertainty rise, and their levels of resilience start to erode. As we saw earlier, measuring and acting mitigates the build-up of stress pollution, as the progression to the state of burnout (mega stress) and shattered resilience is a slow journey. At the time of writing, this has been magnified by the pandemic, and the subsequent changes in hybrid working arrangements and workplace expectations is compounding it. Because of external competing factors the level of awareness can easily slip under the radar. This reason alone is valid for measuring the psychosocial safety in your business. Equally if not more important, the reason to measure is to raise your awareness in a safe and timely way so you can act on the data and not on your feelings, others' assumptions or the rumour mill.

I recently spoke to a colleague who is working on a major project that I did some early work on. Major projects take a significant length of time from conception to approval; planning and commencement of construction can be years apart. The phone call was a courtesy relationship maintenance call to check in on progress. When I asked him how the project was going, he told me that morale was down to about 20% because a senior key leader had left. The replacement person was a *manager* not a *leader*, and the focus went from enthusiasm about seeing the vision and working towards outcomes to being process-oriented and compliance-report-driven where interactions are transactional and not transformational. I asked him if he should be measuring psychosocial safety. He said:

> Remember we are talking about engineers here, and with them if you don't measure it, it's not real. It needs to be measured, so they know if they have to do anything. They work on data and not on opinion.

A valid summary I think of the value in putting science behind the culture so it becomes more than opinion – it is evidence based.

Identifying and implementing

Measuring psychosocial safety is more than ensuring you are compliant with codes and regulations and if you are ISO-certified compliant with the standards; it is a positive step in being proactive in identifying and implementing changes needed. You have a continuous improvement process. This will enable you to remeasure the effectiveness of your improvement strategies and know the levels you have achieved. Imagine being able to state in your annual report an additional safety metric; that of psychosocial safety. The mitigation of adverse workplace social factors and an increase in employee mental wellbeing.

" Imagine being able to state in your annual report an additional safety metric, that of psychosocial safety and the mitigation of adverse workplace social factors and increase of mental wellbeing.

When the survey has been completed, and the feedback from the reports is given this can be both enlightening as to the aspects that are being done well and confronting when there is a significant area of concern. As is a theme through this book, the process is one built on no-blame. The focus of providing feedback is not about what is wrong, but what can be improved, and exploring approaches and behaviours that will be able to be comfortably and effectively applied by the leader through developing a BALL© Plan (**B**ehavioural **A**ction **L**eadership and **L**earning), which we will expand on in the next chapter.

This is not a cookie-cutter approach; the improvement discussion is a positive and creative conversation about what can be done with a level of ease and comfort and what is a challenge for the individual, discussed with a wellbeing focus. The last thing you need is for it to not be done properly and the session creating anxiety and stress for the leader. The BALL© Plan is a collaborative workplace-focused and negotiated approach where the leader can identify areas of their own behaviour that are their strengths and where they can work to adapt this behaviour to accommodate the feedback and mitigate any potential identified hazards. This collaborative approach to changing behaviours and therefore the hazard reduction will be willingly adopted and readily implemented as it is a negotiated approach based on solid data and capitalising on leadership strengths.

It can also be fun. Let me tell you the 'pineapple story'.

I was called in by a Queensland Government department to conduct a mediation session. Basically the Head of People and Culture, Belinda, did not have respect for one of her team members, Ashley. Ashley worked under a flexible work arrangement which had been negotiated with Belinda's leader while Belinda was on extended leave. On her return, Belinda was uncomfortable with the arrangement and decided to stop talking with Ashley, under the premise that *she is never here*. Belinda, a micromanager, decided that the best way to ensure tasks were completed and to enable her to track everything, was to send all instructions and communication to Ashley via email. Belinda's reasoning was that she could track, read *micromanage*, Ashley and therefore hold her accountable for her work.

As could be predicted, Ashley not only found it challenging trying to interpret the exact intent and outcome or output required by Belinda, it also presented a multitude of email trails consisting of questions. This cumbersome process resulted not only in significant delay of work because of the time it took to ask questions and gain timely responses, but also a request by Belinda to her supervisor to put Ashley on a performance improvement program. The reason proposed was that Ashley was not meeting the predetermined timelines for the tasks asked of her. It was at about this juncture that I was asked to conduct a mediation. The process and contents of the mediation remain confidential, except to say that Belinda and Ashley had stopped communicating well for so long they found they didn't know when a good time was to meet to clarify information, and when they did meet they couldn't effectively talk. They would misinterpret words, and either treat each other with silence or shout and then not reach any agreeable solution.

> " This is an illustration that a solution is not too hard to implement, and it doesn't have to be complex, it just has to work for the parties involved.

This was a rather sad case of absolute breakdown in communication. It needed to be resolved, and Belinda's supervisor asked me to mediate as he could no longer work out who or what was right or wrong and had no concept of what could be done about it to 'fix it'. Following a four-hour mediation session, resulting in Belinda and Ashley talking with each other, not at each other, they recognised that this was a tentative step in a long rebuilding process. They agreed on a unique approach which I call a keyword strategy. They called it the 'pineapple strategy'. A simple word was agreed as a trigger for them to use. It was 'pineapple'. If either one of them was having a bad day, a small toy pineapple would balance precariously on top of their computer screen, relying on the strength of Blu Tack to stay there. Additionally, written into the agreement was a commitment that if they were having a discussion and the conversation was starting to become unsafe for either of them, they would say the word 'pineapple'. This word served not only to raise the awareness of the direction of the dialogue, but to break the flow of the conversation so they could agree to take a break, either a short one or a delayed one, and continue the next day. A review after six months identified that the pineapple was the best intervention they'd had, as there was common understanding as to its purpose in the early days of using it and it serves as a reminder of how far they have come in building their communication and working relationship. They now laugh over the pineapple, however it remains a strategy that they feel comfortable with. This is an illustration that a solution is not too hard to implement, and it doesn't have to be complex, it just has to work for the parties involved.

What is sad about that particular meditation is that if the government department involved had conducted a SHEPS or similar review they would have been able to identify earlier that there was a communication challenge. Acting on the information would have enabled strategies to be developed and implemented to prevent the complex breakdown of communication and workplace relationships, and avoided the interpersonal conflict escalating to the level it did. I challenge you to reflect on this situation and consider not only the impact of this situation on both Belinda and Ashley's wellbeing but also that of other people in the section, including Belinda's supervisor who admitted he no longer knew what to do. Sometimes it is much more complex and the following legal case shows us how complicated it can be.

The case of *Workers Compensation Nominal Insurer v Hill* [2020] NSWCA 54 , concerning the death of a home-based employee, reminds us that the boundaries between work and home have become interchangeable. This case was successful as the work-from-home environment was deemed unsafe and the decision upheld by the New South Wales Court of Appeal. The responsibility to ensure the safety for those employees who do not follow strict or traditional hours of work and work late nights or on weekends to complete work is equally if not more important to assess.

Let me now switch to the private sector for another interesting insight. It involves a national company whose CEO engaged me to undertake a SHEPS assessment. There had been some changes in the leadership structure, including promotions and recruitment of new people to the business, and the CEO was prompted because of the changes to do an assessment and gain some baseline data. When we administer the SHEPS assessment, we send an email to employees with a link to the questionnaire. At the bottom of the email there is an invitation to the participants encouraging them to contact me and giving the number if they have any concerns or questions. I had several enquiries from employees as to what confidentiality meant and the extent that they could rely on it. This was very concerning, and indicated perhaps all was not good in the company. Based on the conversations it would appear that one of the executive leaders was stepping outside of her role and advising that she would be collecting all of the responses that were submitted by the staff. She was the leader of several teams in the organisation and it was well known that her need to know everything that was happening in all areas of the business extended beyond what any employee would think was reasonable. The behaviour displayed by her appeared to border on paranoia, where although she displayed a resilient exterior when engaging in communication, her responses would always be on the defensive, sometimes even verging on hostile. She showed little ability to compromise and she found it difficult not to hold grudges. It was my role to reinforce that nobody in the company could or would see the individual answers, and only I had access to the system that held the raw data. The questions from the employees, however, showed me immediately that there were potentially psychosocial safety behavioural challenges with one of the leaders.

It is these early indicators that are not on the questionnaires or may not be heard by other people that speak loudly in relation to the social and mental wellbeing of a business, and where its culture sits. These interactions provide a fundamental insight into the reason SHEPS is so important. It shows how sometimes you don't know what you don't know, and SHEPS provides an opportunity to find out. One of the reasons you don't know is possibly because you're unaware of some of the covert behaviour. Fortunately the CEO was committed to the process and BALL© Plans were developed for the leaders so a structured process of improvement could commence with a positive focus.

The importance of taking action

What is critically important about making the decision to measure is there must be an equally strong commitment to act on the data. To measure is sending a signal that you care, you want to know your employees' opinions – you are saying to them that their opinion matters and is valuable. Asking for their participation is indicating to them you recognise they have an opinion and you would like them to express it. In sending this message it is important that they know they will be heard and importantly their requests genuinely considered. To undertake the process and *not* act on the data is setting your employees and subsequently your business up for productivity loss and potentially the departure of key team members. If you do not follow through, your lack of action will be reflected in your strategic goals and the prospect of them not being achieved is increased. Why? The care factor – because the employees' expectations developed around your commitment to act on their input have not been met. They are likely to interpret your lack of action as evidence that you do not care and their involvement in the survey as 'lip service'. This will result in employees developing a feeling of being undervalued, resulting in decreased morale and an approach to productivity that reflects, *if they don't care, why should we?* From a strategic perspective, measurement is an investment, and failure to act does not provide a return on that investment.

" From a strategic perspective, measurement is an investment, and failure to act does not provide a return on that investment.

One of the men I spoke with in my research who works in a large consulting environment told me they do a culture survey every two years, however it appears it is done so as the boxes can be ticked to say that has been done. He said he has witnessed the rollercoaster of expectations play out in productivity. When the survey comes out there is an expectation that there will be commitment to real outcomes, the energy is high and employees are motivated, believing they can overcome any gaps in process, hazards and perceived favouritism and they will be set to achieve great outcomes. When there is no feedback on the results, or there is feedback but no implementation to improve the environment, the employees revert to a compliance culture. This is where he has seen loss of engagement and the employees simply follow the processes and rules:

> They move from high energy to become compliant and almost complacent. This is the opportunity cost of poor leadership, the financial cost of absenteeism and high turnover, and a cost in projects achieving outcomes which are mediocre at best.

To act on the data is showing not only your commitment to having the best culture and safest work environment, it is reinforcing the values you stand by. If all of the results are perfect or close to it, the action is one of celebration in recognition of the commitment from everybody across the business to building a safe and happy workplace. If all is not well, it is time to celebrate what is going well and commit to your employees that you will support all that is necessary to improve and ask for their commitment in return. This collaborative approach is a process of opening the conversation about what is going well and needs to be celebrated and retained. Measurement and the subsequent results provide new knowledge, it is a time for education, reflection, celebration, and most importantly action.

You don't know what you don't know

Sometimes you don't know because your awareness is distracted due to competing priorities, and other times it is because employees are adept at masking. When employees deliberately cover up mistakes, fail to take ownership for shortfalls and try to hide their weaknesses, you know there are unidentified psychosocial hazards within your workplace. These attributes and behaviours illustrate that employees feel it is not safe for them to speak up and expose their vulnerabilities. They are carrying an internal fear of judgment and possible punishment, which they feel is easier to mask than share. The feeling of not being able to speak up creates a weakness in your team culture which is compounded when there are multiple competitive dominant personalities, and several quiet or reserved ones.

This personality differentiator is particularly evident in sales areas that are commission driven, which is the case for Vee. She works in a role where commissions can be a significant value-add to her salary. Recently there was a restructure and her role was split between her old commission-based position and a new focus in the innovation area. The reporting structure remains with the commission role where there is a new supervisor. She said:

> I can't call him a leader, and I don't know if it is because I am an older female but he will talk with all of the other staff, especially younger guys, on a daily basis, and I have to make an appointment to meet with him, then he tells me I have two minutes.

She goes on to ask me if I think this is discrimination or just poor leadership. As I haven't seen the interactions I cannot fully assess the situation, however discrimination is an aspect of poor leadership. Asking her how she manages, she said:

> When I have a time-critical decision in the sales area I have to go around my immediate supervisor and go directly to the GM so we don't lose the job. Then when we win it my supervisor takes some of the credit of securing the contract and claims part of my commission. I can't fight it as he signs the commission approvals.

Hearing this, I asked her if they had culture or organisational safety surveys. Her predictable response was, 'I wish!'

> Balancing team diversity, strong personalities, personal prejudices and bias is not something that comes naturally to most leaders.

Balancing team diversity, strong personalities, personal prejudices and bias is not something that comes naturally to most leaders. Seeing differences and capitalising on them is a way to optimise strengths and a way for employees to opt into areas that are their strengths and by default opt out of some of the areas that are not their strong points, if the tasks are better suited to other team members. This approach not only provides a strength-based team it minimises psychosocial hazards because there is an agreed balance of the role that each is to focus on, and the accountability to deliver. It is not easy to have this as a pure concept, however trying to apply it through consultation with all of the team members is a positive starting position. Let me share another perspective.

I was having dinner with two professional friends of mine at a beautiful Italian restaurant overlooking the Pacific Ocean. The conversation drifted into the challenges of balancing the needs of a business to continue to provide the service clients expected and the wants of the employees. I asked Ray, a director of a firm with offices across the Eastern Seaboard, if he had worked out why so many clients were ringing him on his mobile. He had told me in a previous conversation that clients were complaining there was a problem with the phone system and when they rang the Brisbane office the phones rang out. It turned out that due to flexible work arrangements all the support team were working from home. The phone system was established so when the receptionist wasn't able to answer the phone, the call was automatically forwarding in a predetermined sequence so as to be answered by the first available person. As part of their role the administration team knew they had a responsibility to answer the phone when it rang and to assist the client. They also knew if they didn't answer it would go to the next number in the chain and the first available person would answer. The problem was none of the administration team would answer the calls; knowing the call forward system was in place they thought the next available person would talk with the client. This resulted in calls going in circles until frustrated clients resorted to telephoning the director. His question to me was: 'So how do we manage this, trying to provide excellent service to our stressed clients while committing to a flexible work arrangement?' The answer is multifaceted, like most workplace challenges, however the first thing I suggest was to check how the work is organised, the level of job control and demands, as well as the context in which the work-from-home requests were arranged. As identified previously, managing the implementation of processes and policies for hybrid work arrangements with different workspaces being utilised – home, office, holiday house – wherever the employee is at the time does not change the leadership responsibility. The requirement to provide a safe environment and the option of being able to survey employees to understand where they are at is a solid starting point.

WorkSafe Australia encourages the use of surveys as one aspect of a consultation process and identifies that 'surveys are particularly useful when:

- anonymity is important, this is because anonymous surveys or tools protect workers from stigma or other adverse outcomes when reporting hazards or concerns
- workers are physically dispersed. For example, they work across multiple sites or shifts
- you need to consult with a large number of workers
- workers need time to consider your questions and their response, or
- workers may struggle to understand or otherwise participate in other forms of consultation.'

I suggest that you want your business to be the one that makes the news for the right reasons not the wrong reasons. Measuring the safety of your workplace not only gives you peace of mind for what you are trying to achieve in mitigating hazards, it measures the success you are having. SHEPS measurements also show you specifically the next steps you can take that are targeted and will have meaningful impact in the areas that are most needed. The BALL© Plan is the action plan to make this happen.

What is there not to like about having science behind you being an employer of choice for having the safest workplace and happiest employees?

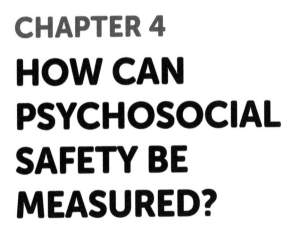

CHAPTER 4

HOW CAN PSYCHOSOCIAL SAFETY BE MEASURED?

The short answer to this is: through a sound and tested structured approach. The long answer is below.

Building a positive culture

Leaders are the windows to psychosocial safety. By measuring leaders' behaviours and the level of hazards within their area of responsibility you will have solid data to show you the level of safety they are applying and the culture they are building. It is both the individual and collective responsibility of the leaders to ensure their workplace is as much as possible hazard free. Absence of psychosocial hazards has a positive impact on your employees' behaviour due to the decrease in stress and increase in a sense of workplace wellbeing. When your leaders build a safe environment your employees will be less likely to focus their energy on having to manage the people and the environment that may have been seen as a hazard. With hybrid work environments that include working from anywhere, the ability of your leaders to rely on their hazard radar has diminished, while the requirement to know if hazards exist – and if so, what they are – has increased significantly. This leaves your leaders feeling somewhat restricted in being able to see the whole employee safety and happiness picture, understand what it means, and recognise if there is a need for any specific action. Like all sound measurement tools, valid data provides an authentic picture for leaders to understand and act on.

> " Leaders are the windows to psychosocial safety.

Building a culture that is based on positive, safe employee behaviour is your ultimate goal. The first step to understanding where to start and how to know that the starting point is the correct one is less clear. You have numerous options, with varying levels of validity and clarity, which means different levels of information for you to act on. Several approaches will be discussed below.

The traditional way to gain employee insights was where effective leaders had systems in place to be constantly alert to potential hazards. They use what I call their Psychosocial Safety and Hazard Radar (PSH Radar). Like all radars, it required a constant state of being alert without being alarmed, active communication, focused listening and conscious observation of your employees as they work through their day. This has now changed with Zoom meetings, work from anywhere, and the increased diversity in workplace expectations from both employers and employees. Your Radar now needs extra support, with solid evidential data.

> The first stage to understanding your employees' psychosocial safety comfort level is to measure it.

The first stage to understanding your employees' psychosocial safety comfort level is to measure it. Measuring provides the validity or otherwise of your radar and puts rigour behind your observations. When it is measured, it can be managed in a focused and structured way. This will enable you to baseline your levels of safety and hazards through data and to act on the collective results you have received through the assessment process. Measuring through an online survey is a very interactive and visual way for your employees to know you care for them. It is also a great way of understanding where your starting point is on your psychosocial safety journey, by establishing a baseline and then building on it.

The actions you take as a result of the data, and that the leaders actively implement through their BALL© Plan, will raise the levels of safety and minimise your hazard score. How does that feel? Just knowing the exact status is the start – implementing actions to improve the score based on the data is the solid foundation that you build upon.

The importance of establishing a baseline through measuring and collecting workplace-specific data has increased over the past few years. This is because the levels of employee resilience are being eroded, and inappropriate and unacceptable behaviours are being played out because of increasing employee stress and anxiety levels. It is evident in the society and business community that we interact with. The signs in the supermarkets and coffee shops and the recorded messages when put on hold for a business call; we recognise that these are challenging times, however we have zero tolerance for abuse or we reserve the right to refuse service to abusive customers. These and similar messages have become entrenched in our daily lives, and they shout volumes as to the increased levels of verbal and physical aggression that is taking place.

The ability of leaders to balance their personal resilience, stress and effective application of emotional intelligence while supporting their employees to do the same is lowering. If left unaddressed, these issues will likely lead to lower self-confidence, reduced productivity, and hindered success in achieving business goals and implementing strategies; however, done well as seen in White's IGA case in chapter 2, there is a significant advantage. They had their radar working overtime and acting strategically they addressed the rising concern before it became a hazard. I have observed, however, that many businesses and the public sector organisations have not, and this is almost becoming a self-fulfilling vortex; the more ambiguity in an employee's role, the higher their stress levels, the more the leader micromanages the employee, resulting in lower productivity from the employee as they believe the leader no longer trusts them to do the job. The longer this continues, the more stress on both the employee and the leader and the lower the confidence and trust in the relationship. The eroding of trust and resilience, as well as a reluctance to discuss the increased psychosocial hazards due to fear of being reprimanded, fear of failure, and fear of feeling foolish for reporting on a friend, are ever present and have a compounding impact not only on the people involved but also their colleagues and work productivity. This is the sad truth.

What I have identified above is only internal to the business; the major external pressures – such as mortgage stress, rising school fees and increased parental expectations – are all contributors to individual employees' levels of stress and anxiety, resulting in unsafe acts and inappropriate behaviour we are seeing in the work environment. Be alert that the root cause of these potential psychosocial hazards is not always evident. That is where non-intrusive online SHEPS measurement becomes your ally.

Confidential data collecting

Conducting a confidential SHEPS analysis ensures strict protocols are followed to maintain integrity and validity of the data collected. Developed to be administered online, the specific and targeted SHEPS survey effectively and confidentially measures the level of psychosocial safety in a workplace through a leadership interface.

So what is the process and how is it implemented?

Following a negotiation with the General Manager, Head of People and Culture and/or other key decision makers in your business, we will agree on a SHEPS Project Manager within your business. This will be your internal go-to person and our communication link. Establishing this single line of communication provides clarity, consistency and a single point for you to understand progress, implementation and improvement. It prevents messages being lost in translation and untruths being spread as I discussed in the chapter above. The Project Manager is also your accountability person, they ensure the commitments from us to you and you to us are honoured through building positive and collaborative relationships.

Working with the designated Project Manager we jointly agree after a review of the organisational chart the specific leaders who are participating in the SHEPS survey. We also identify who the participating employees are – known as 'raters' – and invite them to provide feedback on the behaviours of the leaders, and the extent they are experiencing a psychosocially safe work environment. The raters will possibly have different perspectives, and the questions for the specific business area or department will include the leader's leader, the leader themselves, peers, direct reports and if required people who work with the leader but do not directly report to them. The questions are the same for all. This approach not only gives consistency it provides insight as to the area of influence of the leader and how that influence is being received across the work environment. This approach provides a balance of what other leaders and peers hear and observe in the work environment, and what the employees who work in that area with the leader actually experience, and how the leader themselves believes they are delivering on the people-centred approach to their role. This multi-participant approach minimises bias and provides insight as to whether different groups of people within the business are being treated differently. We spoke about this in a previous chapter where the leaders thought they were being fair and equitable, however their favouritism to the people who they specifically recruited and the bullying of those who they didn't recruit became evident. I am sure you would certainly like to know if this is happening in your business.

Confidential feedback and actioning the results

The SHEPS assessment tool collects and analyses the feedback from the leader and raters, and generates a report that summarises the results. The report shows the leader's strengths and potential psychosocial hazards in their area of influence, and provides insights and opportunities for development and if necessary corrective action. The report also compares the leader's self-rating with the ratings from others. The resultant data shows the alignment or disparity of behaviours or the presence of hazards based on a behavioural frequency rating, and allows for actionable recommendations. The results are very specific and illustrate where there is alignment and agreement and where there is potential that different behaviours being applied may contribute to a hazard.

The leader receives the report and reviews it with a trained coach or mentor. This personal approach is critical for the correct interpretation of the results and provides the support required so the leader will take ownership of the data. The coach works with the leader to assist them in interpreting the results, which are shown as a collective trend and individual group clusters. They then collaborate to create a BALL© action plan for the leader's development. The coach or mentor also provides ongoing support and guidance to the leader as they implement their BALL© Plan and assists them in recognising their progress. This approach is explained further below.

As I mentioned earlier, to ensure the integrity of the system, the survey is founded on years of evidence-based research. It is the integration of the data and leadership coaching and development I have been collecting and monitoring over the past 20 years. This has been done through a combination of observation, coaching, formal and informal surveys, research, and via conducting interviews for culture reviews. I have been directly and vicariously collecting data and supporting information to understand how we can make work environments better – a place where your employees want to be because they are happy to do their work and feel a sense of achievement and impact from what they do, where they feel safe to be who they are and to contribute to dialogue and innovation.

Evidence-based research

Earlier I posed a question about how businesses can effectively measure psychosocial safety in the workplace with the trust of their employees and with full employee engagement in the process. Firstly, let me talk about the *why* before the *how*. Based on the evidence I collected and the discussions I was having with CEOs and key leaders, it became evident that you as business leaders were wanting to know specifically where your business was doing well in managing psychosocial hazards and building a happy, high-performance culture, and what needed to be changed or improved. In doing so, I realised the need to identify where there were areas for improvement in a proactive way to avoid hazards being realised, and that was stronger than your PSH Radar as that was no longer good enough. So thank you to all of the people I have had conversations with and worked with; this is a response to your requests.

In considering the needs, I came to the conclusion that a survey seemed to be the answer, however if it was a general survey the results wouldn't show the specific areas within the business that were performing well or the behaviours, leaders or departments that required specific attention. The general survey result would only allow general action plans, and I thought that was not good enough as the data would not show you where to start if there were hazards to be addressed. With the increase in anxiety across the whole population, adoption of hybrid workplaces, changing expectations of employees coupled with the ever-changing legislative landscape, I realised that neither my psychosocial safety radar nor a general survey were sufficient. In recognising that you need specific, targeted data, I have developed the SHEPS online platform. If you missed it earlier; SHEPS is an abbreviation for the **S**cience of **H**appy **E**mployees **P**sychosocial **S**afety. The questions posed in the survey come from the evidence I have collected from over 200 projects and businesses I have worked with and consulted to over many years.

> When all of the leaders' feedback is combined, the resulting data paints a psychosocial safety picture across your whole business.

The SHEPS online assessment allows measurement to be gained through the targeted approach of assessing the extent a behaviour is applied by the leaders and the degree that the employees feel safe working with the leader. When all of the leaders' feedback is combined, the resulting data paints a psychosocial safety picture across your whole business. This shows you information that wouldn't be gained through discussion and observation.

The online approach allows for the easy identification of trends through data collection and analysis. It provides the opportunity to give written dialogue to support the leader when completing the survey so the leader can gain clarity in specific areas. When more than one survey respondent makes the same comment, it can create a sense of increased credibility that this particular hazard exists and needs to be addressed. It is an excellent and anonymous way to gather feedback from stakeholders at all levels within your business.

The first time the SHEPS survey is conducted in your business the baseline data is established. Depending on the extent of hazards identified – or not – in the base data, we work with the Project Manager to identify the appropriate time to conduct subsequent surveys. This will depend on the extent that the leaders are required to implement a BALL© Plan and their commitment to doing so. If there are multiple hazards identified the repeat survey may be six months after the initial survey, to measure the extent the leaders have worked to reduce the hazards and the degree that the leadership effectiveness has improved. If, however, there are minimal hazards the re-evaluation may be a 12-month cycle. This is a collaborative approach that is business-dependent, as each business is unique with unique challenges and approaches.

The power of the SHEPS report is in leveraging the feedback to identify what is going well and what needs to be done differently, by whom and in what specific areas. The more feedback that comes from multiple employees in various jobs and functions identifying a specific source of stress or anxiety, the increased likelihood that this hazard exists in multiple areas of the business. This then becomes a focus area and the first priority to action.

There are multiple questions in relation to context and self-awareness, job control and empowerment, collaboration and working relationships. When multiple people answer the questions, this illustrates a collective cross-section of feedback. This indicates if the majority of people or just one is experiencing the potential hazard identified and allows the priorities for action to be easily identified.

How it works

Administering the online survey is a confidential and systematic way of collecting data and feedback from your employees, from their peers, from your leaders, your CEO and from your board members to be able to look at psychosocial safety. Most people in these groups are familiar with online surveys and are positively responsive to them. Conducted online from a tablet or laptop, the SHEPS survey takes about 20 minutes to complete. As security, each person is sent an email with an individual link that is specific to them and the leader's area that they are assessing. They click on the link to complete the questionnaire.

The individuality of the link ensures that if a team member is required to assess more than one leader then there is no confusion. This also enables reminders to be sent if the survey is not complete, and also ensures no individual can answer more than once in relation to a leader or section so as to maintain integrity of the results, and mitigate bias in the results.

Using the data

Often if the reports show the presence of significant trends or multiple hazards, the first inclination by the leader that the report is aligned with, is to challenge the findings. This is a natural reaction and often is to be expected. The rejection of the report can be because of multiple reasons – often the leader may assume there is an agenda by employees when they complete the survey, even though they know there isn't. It is a natural self-defence mode that they drop into; and that is acceptable as it is part of the awareness journey. Additionally, we notice when this does happen there is also usually a misalignment in the level of the leader's self-awareness and the level that others think they are self-aware; with the leader thinking they are more self-aware than they actually are. This is one of the many reasons why multiple employees at varying levels of the business complete the survey; it shows you an average of the data, minimises unconscious bias due to there being varying and multiple sources of data, and you understand where your company is at in a particular point in time. It sets your benchmark of your hazards, risks and level of psychosocial safety and gives you the opportunity to improve with a later reassessment. The results give you an opportunity to start developing a structured data informed plan that will incrementally increase your leaders' effectiveness and reduce the psychosocial hazards in the workplace.

The strength of the specific data is your ability to identify and name the gaps that need addressing and the precise outcomes you are looking to achieve. When you specify clear outcomes, you get a return on investment in the wellbeing of your employees, the stability of your workforce and sustainability of your business.

The power in this approach is that everything identified as a possible hazard doesn't have to be acted on immediately. Because of the co-dependencies and the interdependencies of each of these areas, attending to one area has an immediate impact on another. The dependencies mean your employees will notice the positive change and feel grateful for not only knowing that they have been heard, but also that you are acting on the feedback they have given. The feeling of being heard and observing the feedback being acted upon is one of the most important and powerful things for the first step forward. This approach will result in improvements across the board almost immediately, depending on the extent that hazards exist. This very powerful approach to building a mentally and socially safe work environment sets you and your business up for success, not only in retaining competent people and ensuring they are happy – it results in strategic and financial success.

> The strength of the specific data is your ability to identify and name the gaps that need addressing and the precise outcomes you are looking to achieve.

The SHEPS report provides the details of the leaders' self-awareness as measured by the degree of similarity between their descriptions of their own leadership when compared to descriptions through the eyes of their leaders, peers and team members.

The greater the leader's awareness of themselves and their behaviour, the more they can apply their leadership strengths in relation to adaptability, empowerment and collaboration to mitigate psychosocial hazards and meet the needs of the organisation and the people within it to build a positive, happy and safe workplace.

The report identifies the alignment or misalignment of leaders' behaviours as observed by others they work with, and those who have observed them in different specific contexts as well as the teams that report to them. Coupled with a BALL© Plan this solid scientific approach establishes a strong path for building a culture of happy employees. Like all good systems, however, following the process is critical to success.

Process and output

How does the SHEPS process work? It is similar to many of the surveys that you may do, however I think it is important for me to explain it for clarity.

The SHEPS process is usually implemented department wide, or in a medium-sized business for all of the leaders in that business. In collaboration with the Project Manager that we spoke about earlier, for each leader we identify one or two managers they report to, three to five peers and three to ten team members who report to them, each of whom complete the survey. Each invited respondent will rate the effectiveness of the leader in each of the measured attributes and behaviours in relation to the frequency it occurs. They also are given the opportunity to make written statements or comments to support the ratings they have given. The leader will receive a report identifying to what extent their self-awareness aligns with the results from the respondents, and the extent there are psychosocial hazards in their work area as well as how effectively these are being managed.

This whole-of-system perspective provides an insight into the reality of that person's leadership performance and ability to identify and manage psychosocial hazards. Additionally, it identifies gaps to be filled in relation to hazard reduction or elimination, and which specific leadership behaviours the leader may consider using more or less of to contribute to a happier and more productive team.

Raising self-awareness is confronting for those who have not undertaken a leadership assessment and feedback journey in the past. Receiving measurable feedback from colleagues, peers and employees can be even more confronting and challenging, however with the right approach as discussed above, acceptance will develop followed by a willingness to act. This is when you know you have the right leaders willing to work on building a happy workplace.

Specific detailed feedback

When the leader receives their report, the results are presented in multiple ways so they can choose to read the data in the manner that best suits them.

The results are detailed in both a graph and specific written detail to illustrate the areas of strength and those requiring action. This way there is an overall result for the specific leader's area of responsibility. They will be able to reliably understand what specifically they are doing well and what needs to change, how it needs to change and where it needs to change.

The figure below shows a section of the report illustrating Empowerment results. You can see that this leader, who we will call Natalie, had 13 people in her team assess her.

Empowerment	Not at all	Once in a while	Sometimes	Fairly often	Frequently, if not always	n
	0	1	2	3	4	n
I encourage team members to lead themselves.						
Self				3.0		
Average – all raters			2.4			13
Average – rater(s) at **higher** organisational level			2.0			2
Average – rater(s) at **similar** organisational level		1.5				2
Average – rater(s) at **lower** organisational level			2.3			4
Average – 'other'				3.0		5

The results show Natalie thought she encouraged her team to lead themselves fairly often, and rated herself 3.0. Her supervisors (2.0), colleagues (1.5) and employees (2.3) all differed in their opinions. What is interesting is that Natalie's colleagues gave her the lowest rating on this aspect, which tends to mean that when they have observed her working with her team, they believe she does not encourage her team to lead themselves.

The second aspect that is very evident is that although Natalie thought she encouraged her team members to make decisions and carry them out (3.0), none of the employees who worked with her at a similar level in the business believed she did this well (1.5).

There is a similar theme with the other aspects of Natalie's Empowerment responses. This one is asking if Natalie encourages her team members to make decisions and carry them out. The data tells us all the people who assessed Natalie agreed that she didn't do this as much as she thought she did, and that her employees said she did it only once in a while. This shows us there is a high possibility Natalie micromanages her team, which is not only a leadership challenge, as she appears not to encourage them to make decisions and carry them out, but also a potential psychosocial hazard of poor job control. Not encouraging team members to make decisions could be a training development shortfall or a confidence challenge, but left unattended has the substantial potential to become a safety risk. When these results are collectively reviewed with all the other data in the report, it illustrates the extent that Natalie may need to work to improve both her self-awareness and the psychosocial safety in her team.

	Not at all	Once in a while	Sometimes	Fairly often	Frequently, if not always
I encourage team members to make decisions and carry them out.					
Self				3.0	
Average – all raters		1.7			13
Average – rater(s) at **higher** organisational level		1.5			2
Average – rater(s) at **similar** organisational level		1.5			2
Average – rater(s) at **lower** organisational level		1.0			4
Average – 'other'			2.4		5

Following is a snapshot of some of the Empowerment assessment responses. The specificity of this report tells us that without this data the leader would have reported she was effectively leading her team, and her team were empowered to lead themselves, make decisions and carry them out. This data shows that what she thinks she is doing and what is actually happening in the work environment differ. The implication of this, if not acted upon, is that her employees are likely to identify some of the common psychosocial hazards such as low job demand and low job control.

Empowerment	Not at all	Once in a while	Sometimes	Fairly often	Frequently, if not always	n
	0	1	2	3	4	n
I encourage team members to lead themselves.						
Self				3.0		
Average – all raters			2.4			13
Average – rater(s) at **higher** organisational level			2.0			2
Average – rater(s) at **similar** organisational level		1.5				2
Average – rater(s) at **lower** organisational level			2.3			4
Average – 'other'				3.0		5
I encourage team members to make decisions and carry them out.						
Self				3.0		
Average – all raters		1.7				13
Average – rater(s) at **higher** organisational level		1.5				2
Average – rater(s) at **similar** organisational level		1.5				2
Average – rater(s) at **lower** organisational level		1.0				4
Average – 'other'			2.4			5

	Not at all	Once in a while	Sometimes	Fairly often	Frequently, if not always	
Empowerment	0	1	2	3	4	n
I encourage team members' self-belief in their ability and capacity to accomplish a task.						
Self				3.0		
Average – all raters			2.4			13
Average – rater(s) at **higher** organisational level			2.0			2
Average – rater(s) at **similar** organisational level			2.0			2
Average – rater(s) at **lower** organisational level		1.8				4
Average – 'other'				3.2		5
I try to build confidence in team members.						
Self				3.0		
Average – all raters			2.5			13
Average – rater(s) at **higher** organisational level				3.0		2
Average – rater(s) at **similar** organisational level			2.5			2
Average – rater(s) at **lower** organisational level		1.8				4
Average – 'other'			2.8			5

Application and accountability

There is a mountain of research to illustrate that although there are good intentions, 12 weeks after an employee attends a standalone training session, most participants forget 85% of the information delivered. For centuries humans have been aware that experience is one of the best teachers, and reflection is the best way to understand the learnings. For these reasons, the Application and Accountability aspects of the SHEPS Report are critical in decreasing a psychosocial hazard score. And like all safety metrics, attaining *zero* is the best score.

> ...although there are good intentions, 12 weeks after an employee attends a standalone training session, most participants forget 85% of the information delivered.

To attain the elusive zero involves four aspects of:

- acting on the data
- planning and recording (BALL© Plan)
- case study sessions (workshops)
- individual coaching and observation (following the personalised feedback).

Using this approach, leaders will be able to identify the gaps in their team where hazards may arise and identify actions they can take to mitigate the possibility of the risk eventuating. The structure underpinning the process ensures that there is not only a strategic focus on hazard mitigation but also an inbuilt accountability mechanism that the actions are actually being implemented and not just spoken about.

BALL© Plan (Behavioural Action Leadership & Learning)

When urgent challenges arise many leaders, if they have work overload or short deadlines, spend a nanosecond considering the challenge or trying to understand it, and – depending on the challenge – they will make a quick decision rather than investing time in understanding the root cause and working out an effective solution. Many do not ask questions of their colleagues or employees, or make focused efforts to evaluate the resources available to them, human or otherwise. This approach can lead to increased hazards due to poorly considered decisions or not fit-for-purpose answers. Alternatively, if a consultative approach is used without effective focus, and while under pressure to deliver an answer, the leader – while understanding the need for inclusion and consultation – will often allow the outcome to be driven from the activity of the group where the loudest voice will take the lead. The action-oriented ones will champ at the bit to get on and *do something* and those who are reflective are likely to be completely overwhelmed by the noise and confusion in discussion. This less-than-satisfactory approach leads to poor relationships and possibly a feeling of poor support. Both outcomes are recognised hazards that could manifest if left unattended.

Designed to focus on specific aspects of the results of the SHEPS individual reports, each of the leaders will be required to complete a BALL© Plan, identifying the areas they will focus on in their work environment to manage and mitigate the risks and how they will do this, which is done in consultation with the coach who provided the report feedback. The leaders then report to the management meetings what they have done to try to achieve their plan, as a value add to the other leaders who may be focusing on a similar area of improvement. BALL is a work-based plan designed to keep the leaders focused on the application of their commitments to improve both their behaviour and the wellbeing in the workplace while building self-awareness of their abilities and the competencies of their team members. In doing this, the success or otherwise of their actions is what ultimately contributes to your business achieving your *zero-harm target*.

The BALL© Plan is individual to each leader. It is an evolving document recording progress and learnings, based on the areas of focus developed following the feedback of each of the individual SHEPS reports to the leaders. You can see from the example opposite that the implementation process is action oriented and can be adapted to meet the strengths of each of the leaders. This means that even though there may be two leaders who have been identified as potentially micromanaging, the actions they take to mitigate this potential hazard may be different depending on the natural leadership strengths of the individual. The leaders are not alone in trying to implement the BALL© Plans; there is support.

Individual coaching and observation

We do not usually have the luxury of observing ourselves. On the occasions that we do, which is usually on a video, we can be quite taken aback by what we see. What we actually see and what we think we are going to see are often quite different. This is why coaching through observation is such a valuable approach to the mitigation of psychosocial hazards.

Coaching through observation is critical to identifying not only what is happening with a leader's behaviour or within a team dynamic but why it is happening. Recollection through reflection is a fundamental element of leadership development and understanding why a hazard occurred and what can be done to mitigate it. Not surprisingly, staying in observation mode for the leader is hard. When problems are pressing, emotions can work in opposition to rational thought, often wanting to take over at the most inadvisable and inconvenient times, resulting in

BALL©
Behavioural Action Leadership & Learning

Lee Genes
December 2023

Leadership target	Behavioural target	Behavioural actions	Targeted outcomes	Actual outcomes	Learning	Leadership application
Empowerment Micromanaging behaviour. Inability to delegate well. Inflexible nature.	Prioritise workload and delegate tasks back to staff where appropriate. When delegating tasks, have faith in the person to complete the task and be aware of micromanaging this.	**I will:** Prioritise my workload and delegate tasks. **This will be easier if I:** • Do not micromanage the staff I delegate the tasks to. • Develop and apply strategies to ensure the delegated tasks are accepted and completed to agreed standards.	I will have more time to invest in more important tasks relevant to my role. Staff will feel empowered to take on more tasks without pressure. It will build respect with my staff and improve my skills as an effective manager.	Asked HR Staffer to assist with sending me HR forms and info to save me trawling through the system. In my additional duties in my role I was forced to delegate as the team/my staff knew more than I did and I had to rely on them.	Sped up work and made it more enjoyable/productive. Watched another person manage meetings. Very impressive and lots of techniques I can adopt.	With extra duties in my role I quickly learnt who I could and couldn't rely on – there were more than I thought. I felt quite empowered and was surprised how well informed I remained with good systems in place. *I will learn to trust people more in the future rather than being sceptical.* Micromanaging still came out in it all its glory but I felt a 'need' for it to retain control of a situation. I developed a spreadsheet to capture all of the enquiries and made an effort to just casually 'check-in' with staff/team and fill in the spreadsheet. My General Manager really appreciated the spreadsheet however some of my team were obviously threatened by it and made it trickier for me to capture their info. *I will either involve staff in the development and application of initiatives and/or explain the need (mine) and purpose so they do not feel threatened in the future.*
Empowerment Feeling too stressed to allow others to make decisions, thinking this will not be up to standard.	Develop stress management techniques. Understand what is an acceptable standard.	**I will:** Practise stress management techniques to help me manage my workload and staff. **This will be easier if I:** • Work with my General Manager and staff to decide what an acceptable level of standard is and commit to it. • Collaborate with my staff and listen without 'solving' their issues. • Separate the problem from the person when dealing with issues. • Ask my General Manager for feedback on my performance. • Count to ten when things annoy me.	My staff will feel their concerns are appreciated and respect my guidance in resolving them. Help me have a more harmonious working environment.		When I was under a lot of stress I came across as very irritable and my staff avoided me. They had real issues and should not have but thought they were doing me a favour. Genuinely surprised that my experience in the unit has helped reduce the amount of self criticism.	After beating myself up over endless issues I recognised I am my toughest critic and no one is being as hard on me as I am so why worry so much? *Listen to others who identify my strengths and honestly question myself when I am worrying or being hard.* On the first day I asked my manager what her level of expectation was. Two days in I was concerned about the value I was contributing so I addressed this with her, outlined what I was doing and asked if there was anything else? She confirmed all was OK. This helped give me confidence and stop self critiquing every action. *If I am not sure, avoid worrying and ask as the worry may be unnecessary.*

inappropriate actions or decisions. This familiar process illustrates the value of an independent observer who without emotional attachment can provide clarity, not only on the process but the behaviour that was displayed and the impact of the behaviour. Jointly with the leader a new behavioural purpose and outcome may be identified and added to their BALL© Plan if this is the case. Conversely, the leader may be skilled in applying new behaviours, and the feedback from a coach is more immediate than that of the employees who will be processing and considering what in fact the change was. Often the employees feel the change, and will need to do so on multiple occasions prior to understanding and being able to verbalise what it is and the impact on them.

The coaching and observation approach builds awareness that the capabilities developed and understanding gained from the same experience by each leader and team member may be interpreted differently (just as there can be different evidence given by witnesses to an incident). The subsequent application of skills gained may result in different outcomes depending on the *leadership takeaway*. The observation and reflection approach enables reinforcement of appropriate behaviours and negation of inappropriate behaviours by the leaders, such as procrastination, inaction or lack of decisiveness, as discussed above. The learnings from this process are then fed into the leadership meetings and if required specific lessons learned workshops.

Lessons learned workshops

Leadership lessons learned workshops are valuable for leaders to improve cross-company knowledge and effectiveness by learning from their own and others' experiences in implementing the BALL© Plan. It creates a stronger bond in the leadership team and allows for an aligned culture to develop as the ideas and challenges are shared and solutions analysed. The leaders become advocates for and on behalf of each other. These workshops are structured to facilitate a process of the leaders reflecting on their successes and the aspects that they tried and that didn't work, as well as identifying the factors that contributed to them. They share their insights and feedback with other leaders, and learn from each other's perspectives and the practices that have assisted them, and build a culture of learning, collaboration and innovation across their part of the business. When the workshop information is collated the successes show a compounded positive for the whole business or department. These workshops are another measure of the progress of implementation and build a culture of supportive accountability and a way to recognise and celebrate success.

Measurement is the starting point. It provides you with the knowledge of strengths and gaps. It is what you do with the knowledge you gain from the reports that makes the difference.

Data security

With all of the information around cyber security, I feel it is important that you know what protection your data will have.

Our SHEPS system prioritises user privacy with robust encryption protocols and strict data access controls, ensuring personal information remains secure. Your employees experience seamless online interactions while knowing privacy is a top priority. The data is stored in a sovereign environmental system and managed by experienced and accredited professionals. This means you have assurance that your data is only held and viewed by us; it cannot be manipulated, deleted, copied or viewed by unauthorised entities, including the cloud provider.

Implementing the SHEPS program not only provides rich and actionable data that can be benchmarked and remeasured, it allows you to implement your continual improvement strategy to improve the wellbeing of your people. It also shows your psychosocial safety metrics for Section 9 and 10 of ISO 45003, and looks at effectively managing psychosocial hazards and including this management into your continuous improvement cycle.

This approach sends a powerful message not only to your employees but to all of your stakeholders that you care for and about their interests.

Investing in mitigation is better than spending on hindsight.

" Investing in mitigation is better than spending on hindsight.

CHAPTER 5
WHAT IS IN IT FOR ME?

What does this mean for your business? The short answer is happy employees and value creation. The long answer again is explained below.

Value creation

Value is, or at least should be, in the foundation of your strategy; and value is not only found in money, it is in your people, reputation, business sustainability and continuity. According to Roz White, having her 500 employees happy, resilient and feeling safe has made her an *employer of choice*. Steve Rice, CEO of OzeIT, also tries to be an employer of choice because he says he creates *an environment where people are proud to work*.

The increased feeling of wellbeing coupled with experiencing a positive connection with the workplace increases the likelihood of more informed and effective decision making. This is achieved at OzeIT through a collaborative approach in supporting the employees through understanding priorities. This approach provides a task distribution so as to avoid work overload. In practice at White's IGA, the leadership team have been supported to build the core strength of their emotional resilience so they can sustain their personal resilience.

Both of these approaches have been achieved through the open exchange of opinions (all of which are explored), an increased sense of belonging, and includes an increased expression of positive emotions such as happiness. This is demonstrated through positive dialogue and enthusiasm to participate. Roz White told me that, as an employer:

> If I identify and I can see a concern, I have a duty of care to make sure that I'm supporting my employees through that. After all,

you know, they're here working for this organisation. Which I happen to lead. I have a responsibility to look after them. And so when I recognised that, I knew I had to provide some support to help them get through.

These approaches show that supporting employees is providing the value you need to have a resilient and happy business, where people enjoy coming to work. Conversely, as we have been discussing, absenteeism, poor decision making and anxiety can have serious consequences for you and your teams, impacting their performance and the profitability of your business. It is important to identify and address the root causes of the issues, such as workload, work environment, organisational culture or personal factors, and implement effective policies and strategies to prevent and manage them. Absenteeism can reduce the availability and productivity of the workforce, as well as increase the costs of hiring replacements, training and administration.

What doing nothing can cost you

Now I am not usually one for a lot of financial data and other numbers but I think this is worth doing the calculations on. As we saw in chapter 2, the survey by Frost and Sullivan found the financial cost of lost productivity in Australia was an eyewatering $24.2 billion in 2022. That is the financial cost, but what are the health and relationship costs across the workplace, family and community? More and more people are relying on medication to cope, with $635 million spent on mental health prescriptions in the 2021–22 year.[3] The Australian Bureau of Statistics reports

---

3   Australian Institute of Health and Welfare: www.aihw.gov.au/mental-health/topic-areas/expenditure.

that in February 2023, there were 21.2 million people in the usually resident civilian population who were aged 15 years or over, of whom 13.8 million were employed.[4] When you look at those figures, the likelihood of you having one or more of your employees experiencing mental health challenges is extremely high.

> You must be adopting a proactive health and safety culture that ensures your employees work without risk to their physical and mental health and the business is upholding your duty of care to them.

And what does this mean? You must be adopting a proactive health and safety culture that ensures your employees work without risk to their physical and mental health and the business is upholding your duty of care to them. You can look at it from a strategic compliance perspective and say you are working towards alignment with ISO 45003, which is the standard that provides the guidelines for managing psychosocial hazards and risk. From a bigger picture perspective you could also say your business is linking your focus on psychosocial wellbeing to the UN's Sustainable Development Goal 3 to 'Ensure healthy lives and promote well-being for all at all ages'.

That all looks great on tender documents, annual reports and formal documents, but this is about your care factor for the people who are crucial to the success of your business. Or you can look at it from the perspective of some of the data and feedback I have collected. I think it speaks for itself, and I draw your thoughts back

---

4   Australian Bureau of Statistics: www.abs.gov.au/statistics/labour/employment-and-unemployment.

to a comment I made earlier; if you think your employees are not the most important part of your business, try to operate for 30 days without them.

What are businesses saying about the SHEPS program?

Following a consultation process involving almost half of their 1200 people, the employees from PNG-owned telecommunications company Telikom Limited said they were grateful for being able to have their say, felt that they had been heard, and they now have clarity.

Some of the professors and directors of the Thai Nguyen University – one of the four leading Universities in Vietnam – indicated that the SHEPS program raised their awareness that they needed to balance their focus on employee needs as well as students because without the employees they wouldn't have their students.

I spoke with a lady who has been working with international luxury brands that have enjoyed enduring global success for over 60 years. She said they hire for 'will and not skill' because, even if a brand has a long history, 'the brand cannot sustain itself – it is the people who sustain it.'

Every business has a unique experience, and the several tier one construction companies that agreed to be interviewed but not named shared similar experiences – it has changed the way they recruit their project managers and project directors. The focus is 'getting a lot more into the realms of the people side as much the technical', where the safety culture in relation to physical safety has solid systems and procedures but the psychosocial safety is evolving.

There are volumes of research that show highly motivated employees who have job satisfaction will also help to accelerate your profitable growth.

Measure it and manage it

We live in a data-driven world, as seen with the recent upsurge in the use of AI. However, there remains the saying for improvement *you measure it and you manage it.*

The SHEPS platform is data driven so you can measure and manage. The data you receive in the Leaders' Reports can greatly boost the development of your strategy in improving the happiness of your employees through wellbeing, and feed into your performance management systems. It will help you make sense of where you are now, how your people are feeling and where your leaders are empowering and collaborating to create a happy workplace. It shows specifically where your leaders are doing well and what they could do differently. It will build a system that will feed into your performance development and give you valid data to be able to make decisions on employees who are performing well and employees who need support. It will also give you the insight into specifically targeting where this data will help you create a successful employee strategy following a four-step process in action.

To succeed, every leader needs to understand that SHEPS reports are not about them individually; it is about how they and their teams are collectively contributing to the culture and wellbeing of the workplace. It is how that collective behaviour can make a difference to the business as a whole. The message the entire business must recognise is this is about the culture and how each member contributes to that happiness environment. The data collection is being facilitated through the leaders, and the application of safety practices in the work environment show how often they apply processes for collaboration, empowerment and adaptability. The data shows what is and what will make a difference to establishing an enduring positive culture within your business.

The challenges of flexible work and creating a safe environment

What about hybrid work environments? Yes, this does work for hybrid work environments; the aspects of consultation, isolation and flexibility are all assessed, and it can be identified if they are being implemented in a safe way or if action needs to be taken.

Work-from-home arrangements appeal more to established employees with spacious home offices and young children, according to an article written by Steve Mollman on 27 November 2023 for *Forbes* magazine. There are conflicting benefits and challenges in this space. Research conducted by Western Australia's Edith Cowen University published in September 2021 found:

> Implications of remote working to mental health and well-being can be summarised as a balance between the potential negatives of social isolation, work family conflict, technology, transitions to 'normal' working arrangements and the potential benefits of flexibility and connection ... the company of their co-workers was what they missed the most.

I will remind you that this is not a book designed to provide you with legal advice, however there are useful legal precedents. *Ms Natasha Fyfe v Ambulance Victoria* [2023] involves a mother who was doing shift work and requested to change her start and finish times to accommodate her young family. The reason this case is so interesting is it shows that the onus is on the employer to demonstrate that they have given proper consideration to the personal arrangements of the employee, if they genuinely tried to reach an agreement, and if they reject the request they must have genuine reasonable business grounds to do so.

'Reasonable grounds' can be challenging to consider, however the case of OzeIT illustrates it can be done. One of their team members was feeling disconnected from his extended family who lived outside of Australia, but he did not have a significant amount of accrued annual leave to take an extended holiday. The team member discussed this sense of family isolation and disconnect with Steve, the CEO. They came to an agreement where the employee went overseas to see his family for five weeks; week one was a week's holiday. And then he basically worked from home for three weeks, enjoyed another week holiday over there with his family and then returned to Australia to work in the office. Steve said they were both happy with the arrangement because 'he had five weeks with his family, during three of which he worked through the day and spent time with them outside of work hours, and I retained him as an employee'.

The reality check of implementation

The concept of a shift to an empowering culture is a challenge to a lot of long-term employees or long-term leaders. However, once they acquire skills in empowering their people, not only do they yield better outcomes from the employees, but leaders also discover they have more freedom in their own schedules. This allows them additional time to concentrate on strategic aspects they previously believed they lacked time for, often deferring these tasks until late at night when they lack energy after their kids have gone to bed. Often your key leaders perceive this time as quiet, assuming it's the only opportunity they have to focus. This is not quality focus time as their energy levels are low and the actual time taken to do what they want to do is significantly more due to their fading energy levels. The focus time will become available within working hours once they are able to realign their leadership practices and are equipped with the skills to empower their employees.

> The concept of a shift to an empowering culture is a challenge to a lot of long-term employees or long-term leaders.

If adaptability, collaboration and empowerment are not natural behavioural traits, they can be learned with the correct support. Coaching coupled with the BALL© Plan will enable an ongoing strategy to increase the leader's focus and help them to understand that it's a journey. A journey that their team will help them with, their colleagues will help them with, and if they're open to that transition, the whole of the business will provide insights and support. When faced with challenges, leaders tend to revert to their innate behavioural traits. However, having a coach or mentor for support - knowing they are nonjudgmental and understand the experience - provides an opportunity for leaders to realise that mistakes occur and are acceptable if recognised and addressed appropriately.

The first stage in increasing self-awareness and self-confidence is receiving constructive feedback, accepting it for what it is, and being able to act on it in a positive and proactive way. Asking good questions is critical to ensuring that you are shaping a happy workplace, and this is about being able to ask questions openly and building trust. Scott recognises that:

> It's new people who have come in who have the most culture shock. Whether they are coming from a worse place or a better place or whatever the difference is, they're the best barometer because they are not the frog in the boiling pot that has been there for six years. This serves as a powerful reminder to listen attentively and broaden our perspectives beyond those deeply ingrained in our business. They may not be as susceptible to the 'boiling frog' phenomenon, where our working conditions slowly decline and employees adapt without noticing or speaking up. The gradual acceptance may make employees unaware of the changes, leading them to stay despite it sliding from unsafe to toxic.

Among the gold nuggets that I have spoken about, honest uninhibited feedback is also in that pan. It is very valuable, however like gold its value is only realised when something is done with it. If it is not acted on then the consequences are sometimes more dire than we had anticipated.

When the law does step in

In an article by lawyers Joel Zyngier and Maddison Harrington, they report on how WorkSafe Victoria successfully prosecuted Court Services Victoria over its failure to provide a safe workplace and address bullying, which resulted in the death of a senior lawyer of the Coroner's Court.[5]

---

5   www.mondaq.com/australia/employee-rights-labour-relations/1384938/worksafes-watchful-eye-employers-on-notice-regarding-psychosocial-health-and-safety-risks.

One of the multiple reasons that this case is significant is that the workplace was aware of the toxic environment and they failed to act. It tells us in a very strong way that having the information is not enough; we need to act on the information. Acting means doing something with the results of the survey that show where the hazards exist. Is it this simple? Yes, it is. The reports show the results, and the BALL© Plan translates to results into behavioural expectations.

You can research the case if you are interested. The court ruling was that 'his employer was negligent and breached its duty of care by failing to take reasonable steps to prevent or stop the bullying and harassment. The employer did not have an effective anti-bullying policy, did not investigate his complaints, and did not provide him with a safe and supportive work environment.'

Minimising litigation risk

Having a system to identify, evaluate and control risks, and a way to review those controls, must be beneficial to your business, as is illustrated above. The Federal 'positive duty' legislation, enacted in Australia in December 2022, requires employers to take 'reasonable and proportionate measures' to eliminate sexual harassment and other unlawful behaviour from occurring in the workplace, particularly those relating to sex-based discrimination, harassment and victimisation. This is saying that employers are required to be proactive and actions are to be meaningful in the process of preventing unlawful conduct from occurring in the workplace or in connection to work. Taking preventative action will help to create safe, respectful and inclusive workplaces, because simply responding to complaints when they arise is no longer considered acceptable practice. A regular SHEPS measurement is a demonstrated proactive approach that can provide comfort that you can identify the exact areas to target, which means it will be commencing meaningful action. Implementing and evaluating the impact of the BALL© Plan can contribute significantly to providing a safe and supportive work environment.

> " Analysing your across-company SHEPS report will give you a rich source of insight that will identify the gaps between where you thought you had the ideal culture and where you might have psychosocial hazards. Acting on this minimises your risk.

Analysing your across-company SHEPS report will give you a rich source of insight that will identify the gaps between where you thought you had the ideal culture and where you might have psychosocial hazards. Acting on this minimises your risk.

Empowering your people

With fast-paced infrastructure projects, effective and efficient decision making is critical to ensure the project doesn't stall, because on these projects time is a critical driver. To ensure all team members are aligned, we will develop a project charter which varies project to project and most often includes a focus on the project purpose, values, leadership expectations and sometimes performance indicators.

One of the behavioural expectations is often that decisions are made at the lowest possible level. This provides a sense of empowerment which also creates a depth of responsibility. I was conducting a health check on one of these projects; it was a highway upgrade with a whole-of-project value of approximately $450 million, being delivered by a joint venture consortium. Losing time from poor decision making was not an option. The health check involved two aspects: the online survey similar to SHEPS, with additional design to accommodate the values in the charter, and interviewing a cross-section of employees and contractors ranging from the communications team, plant operators and engineers to administrators. Among the several charter-aligned questions they were asked to respond to was 'were decisions being made at the lowest possible level, and did team members know when to escalate an issue?'

Individually the interviews indicated there may be challenges, and even though the discussions were confidential the employees were careful not to place blame on anyone. When the interview data and the online SHEPS hybrid results were analysed we came to realise there were multiple challenges that were not evident. The results showed that there was an inability to take ownership of problems when things went wrong, to view the challenge from the other person's perspective and to conceptualise why a proposed innovation or solution will or will not be successful. There was also a lack of clarity and therefore increase in frustration in relation to what decisions go back to the designer and what changes can be made and implemented on site. Additionally, it was not clear who the final decision maker was when there was indecision. This data suggested there were aspects that could be contributing to delays in effective decisions being made and therefore lost productivity. Without the SHEPS hybrid and the discussions, this challenge would not only have continued, the potential manifestation into lost time, poor decision making, and elevated anxiety and frustration by the workers increased exponentially the longer the challenge was left unaddressed.

Being prepared to look at psychosocial safety from a whole-of-project perspective enabled the project to identify early where there was a potential hazard and to provide both clarity and a process to mitigate the hazard therefore avoiding any adverse outcomes. If the health check had not occurred, the potential for poor workplace relationships and conflict to develop was high.

CHAPTER 6
WHAT DO
I DO NOW?

When I started to write this book, I asked myself what the purpose was for it. But I realised the real question was a little different. It is not the purpose of the book but what I wanted the book to achieve for you. Then I realised the real question I wanted to help you with, and it is:

> How can business owners have a psychosocially safe workplace with happy employees and not be in the Fair Work Commission or the media for the wrong reasons?

I hope I have answered the question.

By now I am sure you recognise that social and mental wellbeing are vital to your employees' health and performance. You have a greater understanding how work is organised, the social factors at work and the aspects of people factors in your work environment that all contribute to happy employees. You are able to identify what affects your employees' motivation, creativity, productivity and engagement, and how this influences their relationships, communication and collaboration with their colleagues, customers and stakeholders. It is a social factor awareness approach and a mindset focused on the positive. Not toxic positivity but realistic, achievable, practical approaches that make a real and lasting impact.

Asking the question *what do I do now?* really gives you three options: do nothing, investigate more, or act now because you recognise you don't know what you don't know and you would like to find out.

Let's consider those options.

Do nothing

This may be your solution if you already have systems in place and your programs are achieving for your employees what you need to achieve, and you have evidence that they are – that is fantastic. Well done. As you now have an increased awareness, I suggest you really cannot do nothing, but the closest to doing nothing while still taking action is to take on some monitoring. I suggest you listen to the coffee machine chats, the lunchtime conversations and the casual exchanges. Be alert for words around job demand such as 'overloaded' and 'pressured', or alternatively anxiety indicators may include words such as 'nervous', 'stressed', 'not sleeping' and 'feeling overwhelmed', and take notice of how much people are talking about working when others are 'sleeping' or 'gone to bed'.

I suggest you also look for behaviours such as:

- employees sitting by themselves in the lunchroom and not interacting with others
- unusual increases in absenteeism
- avoidance, such as not wanting to be part of team decision making or professional development activities
- work that is lower than usual standard or submitted unusually late.

> These indicators may assist you to identify if an employee is experiencing an emotive state – they may be early hazard indicators that you perhaps should not ignore.

I am not trying to coach you to be qualified to assess your workplace happiness. Different people have different stress tolerances and levels of resilience, and we know what one person can accept as a tolerable level of stress, another person cannot. This is what makes it both fun and challenging working with people. What I am trying to do however is give you a way to raise your Psychosocial Safety and Hazard Radar (PSH Radar). These indicators may assist you to identify if an employee is experiencing an emotive state – they may be early hazard indicators that you perhaps should not ignore.

Investigate further

This book has only referred to some of the potential hazards, what they may look like and what they may mean for you. I have mentioned the codes of practice and ISO 45003. These documents outline in detail your obligations. The WorkSafe Australia website has a model Code of Practice that provides practical guidance on how to manage psychosocial hazards which you can download.[6] They remind you on their landing page that under health and safety laws, you must eliminate or minimise psychosocial risks so far as is reasonably practicable. It is a perfect starting place.

Also, if you are ISO accredited you will possibly have the standard ISO 45003 in your quality assurance system, however if you don't there are numerous websites that will provide insights and where you can buy it. A good starting place is to search for 'ISO 45003:2021 Occupational health and safety management – Guidelines for managing psychosocial risks'.

---

6   www.safeworkaustralia.gov.au/doc/model-code-practice-managing-psychosocial-hazards-work.

Also there are multiple articles in the work health and safety journals that your business may subscribe to or that you can access through online libraries.

There is a third option.

Act now

If the suggestions above are not the way for you or you realise you don't know what you don't know, consider if measuring the social facets and mental wellbeing of your employees is both a moral duty and also a strategic advantage for your business. If so, taking action is both a positive approach to ensuring your employees are happy and a risk mitigation strategy.

WorkSafe Australia encourages the use of surveys as one aspect of the consultation process, and SHEPS is one such approach as it has the scientific data to underpin it. However, measuring mental wellbeing is not as simple as asking your employees how they feel. SHEPS is a reliable, valid and comprehensive tool which can assess the various factors that affect your employees' psychological health and social factors such as stress, workload, resilience, fatigue, culture and leadership. It gives you solid evidence-based data.

The data is provided in an easy-to-read report that specifically targets the areas for action, and it is underpinned with a process that allows action to be taken immediately.

It is readily available to you as a tool that can provide data specific to your business, reports specific to your leaders, actionable insights and recommendations on what can be done now improve your employees' mental wellbeing and prevent work-related injury. The SHEPS program is a solid approach to psychosocial hazard identification and to risk control, where you can identify, measure and mitigate.

I also recommend you use ISO 45003, the world's first international standard for understanding the management of psychosocial risk within your occupational health and safety management system. ISO 45003 is based on the latest research and best practices, and it is aligned with the UN sustainable development goal of ensuring healthy lives and promoting wellbeing for all, at all ages. ISO 45003 will help you to:

- identify and assess the psychosocial risks that can affect your employees' mental wellbeing, such as work pressure, role conflict, job insecurity, lack of autonomy, poor communication, harassment, discrimination and violence

- implement effective measures to eliminate or reduce psychosocial risks, by providing clear expectations, feedback and recognition, ensuring fair and respectful treatment, fostering a positive and supportive work environment, and offering flexible work arrangements and employee assistance programs

- monitor and evaluate the impact of your actions on your employees' mental wellbeing, by using surveys, interviews, focus groups and other indicators, and involving your employees in the process

- continuously improve your performance and demonstrate your commitment to your employees' mental wellbeing by reviewing your policies and practices, seeking feedback and suggestions, and communicating your results and achievements.

By using SHEPS and ISO 45003, you will not only set the foundation for measuring the mental wellbeing of your employees, but also have the structure to build the happiest workplace.

This will see you benefit from improved employee engagement, retention, loyalty and satisfaction, as well as reduced absenteeism, turnover and costs. Moreover, research shows that you will gain a competitive edge and a positive reputation in the market, as well as comply with the legal and ethical obligations of your business.

> By using SHEPS and ISO 45003, you will not only set the foundation for measuring the mental wellbeing of your employees, but also have the structure to build the happiest workplace.

The SHEPS platform is a data-driven approach to measuring what's going on with your people in your business. And once you get that data, you can work with us to be able to implement a bold behavioural plan that will help your employees focus specifically on what they need to do and where they need to change behaviours, and also on what to retain because it's working well. Measurement of specific data has a compounding effect; you will see an increased return on your investment because investing in your people gives short- and long-term value to your company.

This approach will provide you with a psychosocial safety scorecard to assess and access the psychosocial safety levels in your business and be able to report this to your board of directors and other stakeholders in your annual report.

Don't wait any longer. Take action today and measure the mental wellbeing of your employees with SHEPS, and then you will actually know.

Our purpose is to work with you to make your workplace a happy one.

Email: sheps@org-cd.com
Web: www.org-cd.com/sheps

Would you like to share?

It never ceases to amaze me the number of people who have experienced challenges in the work environment, and those who have had great mentoring within a positive psychosocially safe workplace. Has reading this book made a difference to you, your behaviour or your workplace practices? If you would like to share, I would enjoy hearing what impact my work is having for individual people and within the business community. I would like to know what difference it made to you as a person and what you might have found insightful.

If you would like to share, please email **sheps@org-cd.com**.

Thanks, Brenda

Would you like to hear Dr Brenda give a presentation?

If you have found this book as insightful as we think you would have, why not ask Dr Brenda to present to your staff, colleagues, industry partners or at your conference?

If you would like to concentrate on a particular aspect of leadership or psychosocial safety, Brenda has been working in this field for decades and brings a uniquely practical approach to understanding, identifying and developing transferable knowledge. It might be about the mindset, skillset, leadership or what to be alert for in the work environment that is hiding in plain sight. Developing a presentation either face-to-face or virtually, Brenda allows time for questions and answers and can tailor a presentation to suit your needs.

If you'd like to know more about doing this program individually or as part of a group, please drop us a line at **sheps@org-cd.com**.

WWW.ORG-CD.COM

Would you like to workshop the SHEPS concepts?

Developing and delivering interactive workshops over the past 30 years has evidenced to Dr Brenda that working with the concepts, debating thought patterns and trying to apply theory in practical settings increases knowledge and skills exponentially. If you found yourself relating to the concepts and case studies in *The Science of Happy Employees: what it takes to have a psychosocially safe workplace with happy and productive employees*, but are unsure how you can apply them, I encourage you to have a workshop to debate and work through the concepts. Brenda's ability to stretch your thinking and empower you with holistic systems thinking and logic, as well as realistic skills in practical application, is unique. Attendees at the SHEPS workshops say they feel less anxiety about having the difficult conversations and approaching staff when they think the person is struggling.

To discuss arranging a workshop, or attending a collective workshop, reach out to us at **sheps@org-cd.com**.

WWW.ORG-CD.COM

There are coaches and there are exceptional coaches

With an innovative approach to behavioural and social change, Brenda's approach is based on the idea that, within a business community, some individuals engage in unusual behaviours allowing them to solve problems better than others who face similar challenges, despite not having additional resources or knowledge. She uses this unique approach within a structured coaching framework so you can see how your leadership strengths can be applied differently to achieve the goals and outcomes that otherwise seem insurmountable or out of reach.

If you would like to discuss further how you can benefit from coaching with Dr Brenda, reach out to us at **sheps@org-cd.com**.